TREEHOUSES OF THE WORLD

TREEHOUSES OF THE WORLD

TREEHOUSES

BY PETE NELSON
PHOTOGRAPHY BY

RADEK KURZAJ

ABRAMS, NEW YORK

Introduction

I started the organization that has come to be known as the Treehouse Conference in 1997 with friend and fellow treehouse builder Michael Garnier. Since then, we have watched the interest in treehouse design and construction grow into a phenomenon. There have been feature stories in the *New York Times,* the *Wall Street Journal,* and *USA Today,* and coverage in magazines including *Time, Smithsonian,* the *New York Times Magazine,* and *Inc.* Numerous books on treehouses have been published (three of which we have authored). We have appeared on TV programs such as *Oprah* and *Good Morning America.*

This interest is not just limited to the United States, where our company, Treehouse Workshop, Inc., is based, and where access to affordable building materials and means of construction is perhaps greatest. We've received calls and letters from folks seeking knowledge about treehouses in countries all over the world. Some have had us over to do the work for them—we were hired to conduct workshops in Montegi, Japan, for instance, and have built in Munich, Germany, and Saltspring Island, British Columbia, Canada. In recent years other treehouse-building companies have been launched, such as John Harris's Treehouse Company in Fenwick, Scotland.

At this year's Treehouse Conference—the gatherings are held at Michael Garnier's Out 'n' About Treesort in Cave Junction, Oregon—there were forty-five people in attendance, coming from cities across the United States, as well as from Japan, Germany, Australia, the United Kingdom, and Canada. It was an international crowd, as it often is. Together we enjoyed photographs, drawings, and stories of work done throughout the year, and we tested some important new technologies. For many of us, though, this year's meeting was especially significant because it reaffirmed what we've always believed to be true: the fantastic allure of being up in a tree refuses to recognize cultural or geographic boundaries, just as it renders age and gender irrelevant.

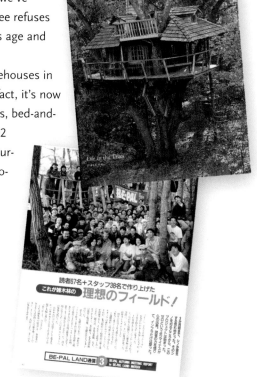

Today, one can use the Internet to find information about treehouses in Asia, Africa, Europe, North and South America, and beyond. In fact, it's now possible to travel around the world staying only in treehouse inns, bed-and-breakfasts, and hotels. Over the course of several months of 2002 and 2003, we embarked on a journey to prove, perhaps only to ourselves, that it could be done. Along the way, we visited and photographed the more than thirty tree structures, both public and private, presented to you here; they have been built in some of the most unlikely locations by some of the most unlikely people. Friendships were formed, ideas were exchanged, and in the end, the world community of treehouse enthusiasts was vastly expanded. Treehouses, as they always do, had united people.

ABOVE: *Treehouses hit the big time when Suki Casanave's treehouse article made the cover of* Smithsonian *magazine in August 1997.* **OPPOSITE:** *Press coverage of treehouses has been hot and heavy over the last several years.*

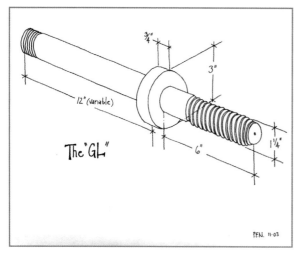

Charlie Greenwood is what some would call an engineering guru, and he has always been a major contributor to the Treehouse Conference meetings. Greenwood's involvement with treehouses extends back to 1994, when his friend Michael Garnier, owner of Out 'n' About Treesort, hired him to consult on work being done at Out 'n' About. Greenwood is the engineering mind behind the design of a device known among Treehouse Conference attendees as the GL, what is unquestionably the most important technology to come out of the Treehouse Conferences since we started the organization in 1997. (*GL* is short for Garnier Limb, as the device was developed due in large part to the efforts of Michael Garnier.)

Our main objective at the Treehouse Conference has always been to educate the participants about the latest developments in treehouse-design and treehouse-construction technologies. The conference has also been a productive forum for conducting hands-on tests of new ideas. Besides treehouse designers, builders, owners, and other enthusiasts, engineers and arborists are always present. Each year in October we gather at Out 'n' About and try to move the ball further down the field. Throughout the conference's seven-year history, though, the primary focus has definitely been how best to connect the treehouse to the tree.

The GL is a turned-steel limb, a human-made hardware device that looks like a billy club with a donutlike disk, or collar, attached to it a few inches off center, the lesser end threaded like an ordinary screw. By screwing it into a tree trunk just right, until the collar is tight against the trunk, an immensely strong structural support limb is

created, which in the right kind of tree is capable of carrying the weight of, say, a Ford truck. The design of the GL has been continuously refined and retested year after year at the conference, to the point where it is today, capable of sustaining nine thousand pounds. With it we can safely put larger structures in trees without losing sleep at night.

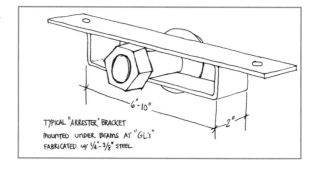

TYPICAL "ARRESTER" BRACKET
MOUNTED UNDER BEAMS AT "GL's"
FABRICATED w/ 1/4"-3/8" STEEL

OPPOSITE, TOP: *The "GL" is the most important advancement in treehouse technology since sawn lumber.*
OPPOSITE, BOTTOM: *The "arrester bracket" attaches to the bottom of the beam and allows the tree to move in high winds. The nut prevents the bracket from sliding off the end on the GL.* **ABOVE:** *Here is a GL in a large western red cedar tree. We tend to back up larger loads with a cable-and-turnbuckle system that attaches to the end of the GL and is anchored with a large lag bolt positioned four feet higher in the tree.*

Chapter 2 *The Workshop*

PERHAPS THE BEST WAY TO GO ABOUT OUR TREEHOUSE TOUR IS TO START WITH A QUICK WORKSHOP. THIS WILL ALLOW US TO LOOK WITH A MORE INFORMED EYE AT THE TREEHOUSES PRESENTED IN THIS BOOK. FIRST, WE WILL LOOK AT THE KINDS OF MATERIALS THAT TYPICALLY GO INTO A TREEHOUSE. THEN WE WILL CONSIDER THE DESIGN AND CONSTRUCTION PROCESSES, SHOWING SOME VERY REVEALING PHOTOGRAPHS OF AN ACTUAL TOP-TO-BOTTOM TREEHOUSE CONSTRUCTION. LET'S DO IT.

MATERIALS

One of the most enjoyable aspects of treehouse building is the process of finding and collecting materials. Anything goes here. While it's very important to keep in mind the importance of selecting only the strongest materials for the platform, one can and should have fun selecting materials for what is built from there. The possibilities are practically endless.

The platform and joist materials (for more information on joists, see the span chart on page 216) must be built with good solid wood. Reclaimed timbers are fine, in fact preferred, but be sure they are in good shape—watch for cracks that run all the way through the timber. Also avoid timber with a large number of knots.

Here in the Pacific Northwest where we live, we have the luxury of being in the middle of America's timber country. While they are getting harder and harder to come by, deconstruction sites exist here as old buildings are being torn down to make room for new construction. My partner in Treehouse Workshop, Inc., Jake Jacob, has been making a living for years dealing in reclaimed building materials. Reclaimed materials have in fact become big business in the United States as more and more people discover the beauty in the patina of weathered wood and steel and the personal satisfaction inherent in rescuing these often perfectly reusable materials.

Most metropolitan areas have a store that deals in reclaimed or salvaged building materials, too. Often it's the unappealing stuff that is the most visible at such places, like old toilets and aluminum windows, but there always are a few gems hidden in the stacks. These can be great places to pick up old wood windows and doors, for instance. Another place to look is in the classifieds section of your local newspaper under "building materials." Along with such items as used bricks and sheets of tempered glass, sometimes one can find advertisements for old barn siding, odd-sized timbers, and leftover plywood.

Jake has done such a good job of converting me to reclaimed materials that, much to the chagrin of my building inspector, I chose to build my entire house with the stuff. For treehouse construction especially, reclaimed materials ought to be the rule.

Stacks of wood at the workshop in Fall City are ready to be put to use. I must admit that I am becoming a bit self-conscious about becoming a pack rat and driving down the property values in my neighborhood, but I just can't help it. All this stuff turns into great treehouses.

Old-growth cedar logs came from a defunct sawmill. Now, with the help of a portable "Wood Mizer" band saw, the logs are being turned into the most beautiful siding and interior paneling imaginable. Old windows being cleaned and repaired.

DESIGN

Designing treehouses is my favorite part of the overall process of bringing a treehouse to life. For me, designing is an exercise in building as much as it is an exercise in putting ideas to paper. At this stage, even though you are drawing, you are still building, if only in your mind. In this way, you get the best of both worlds in the design stage of building a treehouse.

Start the design process by getting an understanding of what the treehouse is going to be used for. Is it an extra bedroom, or is it a fully outfitted vacation house? Then, follow these basic design guidelines.

Establish the floor level, or how far off the ground the floor of the treehouse will be. (My designs typically have a floor level of 10 to 20 feet.)

Prepare a survey drawing of the site that reveals the positioning of the trees you will use, measuring the distance between the trunks and branches at the proposed floor level and the diameter and rough shape of the trunks and branches. (Fig. 1)

Transfer the survey drawing and figures onto graph paper, keeping it to scale. (I like to use a half-inch scale, or $\frac{1}{2}" = 1'$.)

Laying tracing paper on top of the survey drawing (or by using a computer application for survey drawings), take a few stabs in pencil at sketching between the trunks and branches a simple system of beams that will support floor joists and decking. If you can, boil it down again to its simplest form. (Fig. 2)

Now subject your sketch to a quick reality check to be sure what you have in mind will work. Take the drawing out to the site and compare it closely to what is before you. Is your platform size adequate, or is it too big? How, then, can the platform be expanded or trimmed back? Do the trees and branches need to penetrate the structure? (In my experience, a truly waterproof structure cannot be created if you allow a tree to penetrate the structure.)

Tanya Jensen, this year's workshop client and the mother of two beautiful girls, sheepishly handed this drawing to me in hopes that it would inspire the treehouse design.

Sketch the design of the undercarriage on a new sheet of graph paper, again keeping it to scale. (Fig. 3)

Consider climatic factors in relation to the positioning of the treehouse as you have it on paper and the actual positioning of the trees to which you will secure it. Where will the sun hit the treehouse and at what times? Perhaps you will want to have cocktails on the deck at sunset? Now is the time to plan for that.

Using tracing paper, start sketching the walls and block out areas for outside decks or covered porches. Will you need a loft or a second story?

Determine the positioning of the entry door and be sure there will be adequate space for a proper landing in front of it.

Now draw your floor plan to scale on graph paper. Indicate desired locations of windows and consider where the main stairs would best intersect with the platform. Do you want a direct approach from below, or do you want to hide the stairs to some degree? Do you want stairs at all? Maybe a removable ladder would suffice? (Fig. 4)

On a separate sheet of graph paper, begin to sketch the elevations of the treehouse. This is what the treehouse will look like face-on when you're done. Your intuition will tell you what looks good proportionally, so let it speak to you.

Work your way around the floor plan to see what the treehouse will look like in two or three other elevations. Work out issues such as window sizes and locations, wall heights, and roof pitches. (Fig. 5)

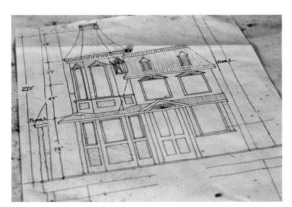

A final treehouse elevation.

Making a crude model of the treehouse can be an extremely helpful tool. It can be used to resolve framing issues that may not come to light in the drawing phase, and it can come in handy when discussing the erection plan.

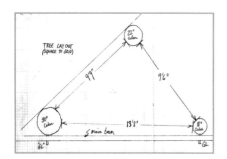

Fig. 1

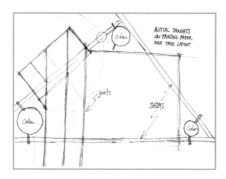

Fig. 2

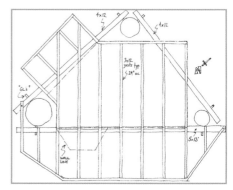

Fig. 3

New ideas being discussed during a design portion of the workshop.

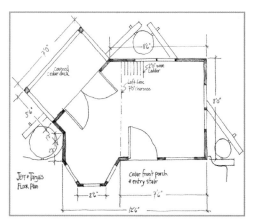

Fig. 4

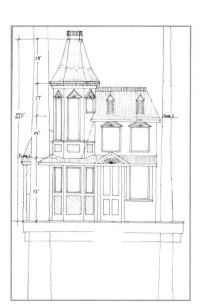

Fig. 5

At this time the many framing issues can be worked out as well. Try to get as detailed as possible so you will be able to build from the drawings you are creating.

Once you are satisfied with your graph-paper drawings of the floor plan and elevations, break out the good tracing paper and trace over your drawings to create the final drawings.

CONSTRUCTION

There's no need to call the excavator and the concrete guy. Our foundation is already in the ground. No wonder I love building treehouses so much! Just break out the drill and the pipe wrench, grab a few GLs, and let's get some wood in the trees. By lunchtime we will have enough decking on the platform that we can have a picnic up there. Such is the beauty of the GL.

During the construction of this treehouse, we had a few extra hands to help us get the work done. Actually, there were twenty-one students in all and five teachers/carpenters. We had five days to build, and at the end of that fifth day, we determined, we were going to have a group photo on the stairs and deck of a completed treehouse, no matter if it killed us! You see, we could sit around and talk about our treehouse, or we could just get out and build it. Here we go.

Ian Jones deftly sends a piece of cedar through the router as he creates ship-lap for the tree- house siding.

Try to leave at least two inches of space between the tree and the decking.

All hands on deck for the raising of the first wall.

INSTALL THE HARDWARE

Pick the point in the tree where your main beams will rest. Perch your beams on top of your hardware as a rule. Do not pin your beams to a tree if at all possible. Allow for independent tree movement and growth.

INSTALL THE MAIN SUPPORT BEAMS

We use a small but strong custom-fabricated steel bracket to keep the beam upright on the GL. It also acts as a wear-prevention plate between the wood beam and the GL, as well as a movement restrictor. (See illustration on p. 8 of "arrestor bracket.")

ROLL THE FLOOR JOISTS

The spacing of your floor joists apart from one another will depend on the material you are using for decking. Typically, for a backyard deck, joists are spaced 16 inches on center. With 2x decking, spread the joist to a spacing of 24 inches. Use rim joists and blocking between joists to avoid having your floor joist flop over onto their long sides.

The windows have been left out of their openings for obvious reasons.

It is another group effort to stand up the second wall.

INSTALL THE DECKING

Be sure to respectfully cut around the trees, leaving at least 2 inches of space. Make a nice cut of it, too.

FRAME THE WALLS IN MANAGEABLE SIZES ON THE GROUND

Frame economically. Don't overdo supports under window sills and door and window headers. You are building a treehouse, not a bank vault.

Finish the exteriors of your walls as much as possible while they are on the ground.

Build your window casing (the trim around your windows) in such a way that the window can be installed from the inside, after the walls are in place and the roof is on. Keep in mind that the window openings make great places through which to run scaffolding when framing the roof.

While the railing is installed by the all-English team of Simon and Graham, Ian and Shane work on the front porch roof framing.

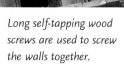

Long self-tapping wood screws are used to screw the walls together.

Bubba leads the tower roof crew with skillful screw-driving back at the shop.

GATHER ALL YOUR ABLE-BODIED FRIENDS AND START HOISTING WALLS

At this point you will want to get a game plan together so the treehouse can be assembled a piece at a time without blocking the receiving area.

Snap some chalk lines on the platform so you know where the walls are to go.

Screw together the walls at the corners first with long, self-tapping wood screws.

Screw the bottom plates of the walls to the platform last.

FRAME THE ROOF IN PLACE

(They often get too heavy and awkward if you try to frame them on the ground.)

WHEN ROOFING, BE SURE TO TIE-IN TO A ROPE SECURED HIGHER IN THE TREE.
START THINKING ACCESS

Now might be a good time to build your stairs (if you go in that direction). With all the details left to be finished, you might appreciate the efficiency of a nice set of stairs.

Jake and Beemer retreating from the roof deck.

Daryl with the long reach on the mansard roof.

Many details came together at once.

BUILD RAILINGS

Make them 36 inches high and space the ballasters in such a way that a 4-inch sphere could not push through.

INSTALL DOORS AND WINDOWS AND TAKE A PICTURE

(I'd love to see it, by the way.) Now it's up to you as to how to finish it out. Heck, you have come this far, why don't you electrify it, insulate, and put up some good-looking wood paneling? Just don't drywall!

The number of days didn't help a lot.

It is fun to see what can be built in five days when you have enough people.

OPPOSITE: *After a driving wind-and-rain storm, we got the picture in.*

I will never forget this photo that appeared in National Geographic of a treehouse in Irian Jaya, Papua New Guinea, where an entire culture lived in the trees! This aerial view shows one of their creations, one that hovers more than 150 feet off the ground.

BOO'S TREEHOUSE *Seattle, Washington, U.S.A.*

A few years ago, we received a welcome call from a local family that wanted to build a treehouse for their teenage daughter. Boo was turning fifteen, and her parents had spoken of building a treehouse for her for some time. Now, they figured, the time had come, and they would call in a professional to do it.

Boo had fantasized about her house in the trees for quite a while, so when we sat down for our first design meeting we had plenty to discuss. It was to be a place where Boo could escape with her friends and talk or have sleepovers. She wanted an outdoor deck to look out over the rooftops of her neighborhood. Most importantly, she wanted a ladder that could be raised and lowered so that she could cut herself off from the rest of the world when she was in residence.

Boo's treehouse was built in the summer of 2002 on a steep hillside in one of Seattle's older neighborhoods, near the campus of the University of Washington. The tiny brick Tudor Revival-style houses that dominate the housing stock of the area offer little room for expansion, and so the only way for this family to add on was to add up—up in a tree.

ABOVE: *Boo's treehouse is perched on a steep hillside in a stunning Diadora cedar tree.*
OPPOSITE: *The back of the treehouse is only seven feet off the ground, but the front is thirty-five feet up.*

OPPOSITE: *Boo's house from the back. There is a retractable ladder so she can hoist it when she wants to be alone.*
TOP: *Re-milled cedar 2 x 12s serve both as siding and as interior paneling. The floor is solid fir 3" x 5" car decking. It spans four feet between joists.* **ABOVE:** *Old windows can be a pain to rehabilitate but they sure do lend character.*

SURFASS TREEHOUSE *Gig Harbor, Washington, U.S.A.*

Miriam Surfass first contacted me by writing a kind personal note requesting that we visit the site of her summer home to assess the possibilities of building a treehouse. I recall how much her letter, written by hand, captured my imagination.

When I first pulled into Miriam's driveway, she was waiting with cookies and lemonade. Her nifty sports car was parked in the carport with the top down. She had only just arrived at the Gig Harbor house, coming here to escape the heat of California, where her other house is located. As Miriam came to greet me, I noticed her foot was in a cast. Soon thereafter, I heard of the car wreck she had been in. She also joked about how fast she drove from her home in Southern California to the house in Gig Harbor, a new personal best. I liked her immediately.

Sited across the water from the jagged snow-capped Olympic Mountains, Miriam's property is stunning. At times, it's a whale watcher's paradise, and it's an area known for its amazingly good oysters. Miriam's family has held the property for generations.

Although a summer or two passed before Miriam's treehouse dream was realized, we finally did it. Now here again as part of our around-the-world journey, I am reminded of how much I enjoyed building Miriam's, and how she is one of my favorite people to have built for.

ABOVE: *Miriam Surfass was looking for a simple place to climb up to and find some peace. She had had the treehouse dream since she was a little girl. Now in her seventies, she also wanted a place that could attract her grandchildren.*
OPPOSITE, TOP: *Miriam's property has been in the family for years. I cannot imagine a more perfect treehouse location.*
OPPOSITE, BOTTOM: *It is a little exposed to the weather, but when it clears up, there is a fantastic view of the snow-capped Olympic Mountains across the water.* **OVERLEAF:** *That's about all you really need.*

SAM'S TREEHOUSE *Purdy, Washington, U.S.A.*

During one of our first meetings, Sam made it very clear to me that he knew exactly what kind of treehouse he wanted. He had a copy of my first book on treehouses, and he turned right to the page of the treehouse he had been dreaming of. Naturally, it was the hardest one in terms of construction that I had ever built, the round house on Saltspring Island in British Columbia, Canada. Sam then pulled out a sketch he had prepared, which noted his simple requests of the design: a place to lie down, a place to write, and some shelves for books. Oh, and if he could have a drawbridge to pull up, that would be great. Maybe a metal roof so he could hear the rain. He plans to use the place to get away and be by himself.

Sam was diagnosed a few years ago with a form of leukemia. Through the extraordinary organization the Make-A-Wish Foundation, Sam had me tracked down and together we set about designing his fantasy treehouse. I was so proud to have such a kind and caring young treehouse fan.

Sam's Treehouse was built in August 2003 by the wonderfully creative carpenter Bubba Smith from Texas, based on the design that Sam and I had created. Bubba created a very unique system of layering 2" x 6"s and 2" x 12"s in such a way that the entire circular platform is only 4½ inches thick. There are no joists, and the entire structure is held up by three GLs. It is an elegant system and is quite pleasing to the eye, though it proved highly labor-intensive, as all the radii were cut out of 2" x 12" fir and hemlock boards. The structure was quite a puzzle to put together, with much head-scratching and gnashing of teeth.

All of the building materials came from donations. The local building-supply store provided all of the lumber used in the platform. Another star contributor provided the resawn salvaged cedar that was used as both the interior and exterior walls. Another supplier provided the larger dimension salvaged fir used in the bridge and stair construction, as well as the knee braces under the main treehouse. The rusty metal roofing came from an enormous dairy barn that our company deconstructed a few years ago.

ABOVE: *Good Sam, hanging at his new pad.*   **OPPOSITE:** *For years, Sam and his brother Joe had been using the treehouse tree for a rope swing.*

OPPOSITE: *It was decided that no treehouse would be complete without a bridge.* **TOP:** *And a ladder that could be raised and lowered. (Notice the concrete-filled ABS pipe hanging as a counterbalance in the fir tree by the ladder.)*
ABOVE: *Here, one can see the detail of the intricate floor system from the inside.*

REDMOND TREEHOUSE *Redmond, Washington, U.S.A.*

Here is a perfect example of how fast your kids grow up. Steve Rondel of Redmond, Washington, had three children grow up before he could finish this exceptional edifice. Now he is looking for grandchildren, so he has an excuse to push on. This all started twenty years ago, when Steve's oldest son was five years old. They had spent some time at Disneyland, and things got started from there.

ABOVE: *Finding a treehouse like this is like finding buried treasure. This one was started twenty years ago, a project by a father for his children. Now he hopes to have some grandchildren so he can have an excuse to start it up again.*
OPPOSITE: *A more ambitious treehouse would be hard to find. Over the course of many years, Rondel spent his evenings and weekends obsessively adding to an ornate plywood palace in a broad-leaf maple tree.*

TOP: *Scrollwork letters in 3/8" plywood makes for beautiful windows; it also represents each of Steve's four children.*
ABOVE: *Stairs climb organically between two trunks to the third of the levels.* **OPPOSITE:** *At one point fairly early in the construction process, one of the four main trunks snapped. Rondell creatively turned lemons to lemonade and promptly craned the massive branch upside down, stuck it in the dirt, and used it to support an even more ambitious third level. Eventually the trunk rotted (note its protrusion from the left corner), and a tripod of heavy metal pipe was installed in its place.*

The treehouse has been used most recently as a haunted house for a Halloween party.

Anything goes when you are in the trees. It is inspiring to see this kind of freedom in design and execution, even though a structural engineer might freak.

LOLLY'S TREEHOUSE *Fall City, Washington, U.S.A.*

Lolly has been a treehouse fan for a long time. After raising two kids and retiring from a busy teaching job at the local elementary school, she started having visions of a treehouse art studio all her own. She wanted a place that was separate from the house, where she could escape and pursue her passion for watercolor painting.

Despite the fact that Lolly and her family live on five acres, and that there were more than a few locations to choose from for building the treehouse, one area—a grove of mature western red cedar, Douglas fir, and broad-leaf maples—jumped out at us. These trees were perfect from all angles; they were healthy, their spacing was ideal, and the outlook to the north and east was exceptional from this spot. The location also had good proximity to the main house (about a hundred yards or so) for power and the all-important bathroom, and yet from the main house, the treehouse would be impossible to detect. The treehouse would have all of the privacy of a small cottage far off in the woods.

Lolly wanted a lot of natural light and windows to take advantage of the fantastic views. She didn't require a large space (the main room is 10' x 10'), but it had to have room for a daybed and storage space for art supplies. She also needed electricity so she could go out there at any time of day or night and a space heater to keep her warm and her papers dry.

In any treehouse design it is important to simplify. Lolly's, built in 2002 by Treehouse Workshop, represents the latest findings in treehouse-design technology. By the time the structure was in production, the GL had become the mainstay in treehouse structural engineering, and it was, of course, utilized here. The GL simplifies immensely the procedure of attaching a structure to its host tree.

ABOVE: *It is a tight squeeze—access is made between the house and one of the main support trees—to get out to the small viewing deck.* **OPPOSITE, TOP:** *The basic structure was modeled after a common lookout.* **OPPOSITE, BOTTOM:** *In the summer, the treehouse all but disappears behind the foliage.*

Nearly all of the materials in Lolly's Treehouse were salvaged and recycled. Only the fabricated metal tree connections and the electrical materials were new. The rest of the 156-square-foot house comprises reclaimed 5" x 14" Douglas fir beams (one 29 feet long!), 3" x 12" fir tongue-and-groove flooring, 2" x 8" cedar decking on the 80-square-foot deck, 2" x 3" fir framing, 1" x 10" reclaimed cedar siding, 1" x 8" salvaged alder for the interior paneling, and reclaimed metal for the roofing. The leaded windows came from the sun porch of an old Federal-style house in Seattle's historic Capital Hill neighborhood.

Originally, Lolly had imagined a "three season" house. Winters are, for the most part, quite mild in the Northwest, so insulation was something she had planned to wait on. As it turned out, however, we were finishing up just as winter was coming on; Lolly enthusiastically made the executive decision to take it to a higher level of finish. After a simple wiring job, insulation was added and the entire interior was paneled with 1" x 6" tongue-and-groove alder. Lolly's Treehouse now heats up nicely with a single space heater.

OPPOSITE: *A view from below shows the wall of salvaged leaded glass windows that command an endless view of the valley and mountains to the north.* **TOP:** *Lolly proved to be quite an interior decorator.* **ABOVE:** *One side of the treehouse has a 7' x 8' pop-out with a shed roof. Lolly keeps her art supplies here, but there is room for a queen-sized bed if they ever decide to use the house as a guest bedroom.*

THE NEST *Yelm, Washington, U.S.A.*

Roderick Romero is a multi-media artist and treehouse architect and builder based in lower Manhattan. His creations reflect his unique view of nature. "It's very metaphysical," he says. "I try to let the tree communicate with me and I communicate with the tree. The tree tells you where to move and what your boundaries are, where you can stress things, and what direction you can go." He is one of these guys that goes with an emotion and then captures it.

Roderick went outside the box on a treehouse he constructed south of Seattle in the private garden of a patron of the arts. He was charged with building a garden sculpture for an all-night summer solstice party that is hosted annually by the client. He calls it the "Nest at Encantado," and it literally hangs in a maple tree. One must climb a cargo net made of fat manila rope to get up the tree trunk, and then across similar netting to get to the pod that is about three feet or so from the tree. The whole structure sways back and forth as you make your way into the cushiony confines of the opposing pyramids. From the soft, regal pillows, one can look up into the rafters and see all kinds of copper and organic materials woven into the underside of the roof. The first thing I noticed was the electric feeling I had as I sat back in the cushions. The fillings in my teeth felt like they were going to jump out of my head! From below, Roderick was most pleased to hear this and then explained that he coiled a 600-foot spool of copper wire around the roof and below on the opposing pyramid.

The most striking visual element of this treehouse is the way Roderick wove all of this wonderful, organic material into the base of the structure. Much of the material was pulled out of a pond on the property: lots of reeds and water grasses, but also incorporated were moss and twigs. When I asked him how long it had taken him to build his beautiful bird's nest, he rolled his eyes and looked a bit embarrassed. He and his building partner, Wolfgang, obsessed for weeks and weeks in the building of his vision. If you count time he spent lying awake at night or dreaming about it, it was pretty much twenty-four hours a day for two months.

ABOVE: *The interior of the pyramid roof of Roderick's "Nest" treehouse is woven with thorns, bamboo yarn, hundreds of feet of copper wire, copper sheathing, and fabric.* **OPPOSITE, TOP:** *Roderick spent weeks weaving plant materials into the opposing pyramid's undercarriage.* **OPPOSITE, BOTTOM:** *Roderick's "Nest" is situated inside the walls of a secret garden. The only entrance to the garden is through this ancient carved wood door.*

ABOVE: *Many more hours were spent splicing big manila rope to form a cargo net-style ladder.* **OPPOSITE, TOP:** *The climb up is followed by a short climb out to get to the inviting cushions of the inner sanctum. Below the cushions is a removable floor that hides more pillows and blankets for overnighting.* **OPPOSITE, BOTTOM:** *A horse's head carved from a glue-laminated beam serves as a strut to keep the one and only support cable six feet off the maple tree.*

ABOVE: *The creative means of ascent resembles a spider web. It is easy to climb and feels remarkably safe.*
OPPOSITE, TOP: *On the opposite end of the garden there hangs another interesting pod, designed and constructed by Seattle artists Glen Herlihy and Branden Zebold. They call it the Copper Cocoon and it is is used as a meditation chamber.*
OPPOSITE, BOTTOM: *The chamber is expertly crafted with a riveted copper skin and, inside, fastidiously joined red cedar. It is suspended only about a foot off the ground and weighs only 140 pounds.*

Pam's Treehouse was designed to be a relaxing getaway—a place to take one away from the worries of the world and a place for magic. To me it seemed that Pam would use it as a place to charm her future husband. She wanted decks to look out upon the fields from a small but comfortable living room, along with a bathroom and a small, intimate bedroom.

Before we began construction work on Pam's getaway treehouse, however, and in fact while we were in the forest going over the design ideas, one of Pam's friends suggested that a second treehouse be built to serve as an office. Within minutes we were back on the opposite side of her property scouting for a good office location. We settled on two large trees that were spaced perfectly to fit a small office treehouse between them. The office treehouse was to be higher than the other, about 15 feet off the ground, and it needed to have just enough space for one or two people to work comfortably.

These two treehouses, both completed in 2001, sit on a stunning large piece of property in the shadow of Mount Rainier. There are expanses of open pasture, in addition to rolling lawns and beautiful formal gardens. The forest is young—mostly second growth Douglas fir trees.

The first treehouse, which includes 320 square feet of interior space and 300 square feet of outside decking, was built farthest away from the main house on an elevated ridge that separates a small pond from a larger pond in the middle of an open field. The larger pond is filled with rambunctious bass that boil to the water's surface every evening. Here the trees are not so remarkable and are at most 14 inches through at breast height. Nonetheless, all the trees were in excellent health. Our biggest challenge here was to get the deck that overlooks the pond properly sized. With all the nicely spaced trees to choose from, it seemed a shame to post down just to accommodate a deck, so we chose instead to create a cantilevered beam off the two trees that were 12 feet apart on the pond side. Bolting to the pond-side face of the trees, we built two beam- and knee-brace systems. Then about 6 feet off the trees toward the pond we mounted a second beam perpendicular and on top of the two

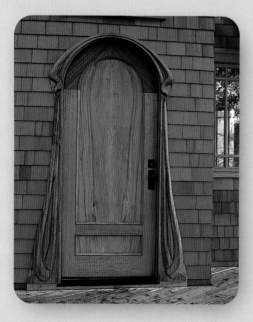

ABOVE: *Not far from the "Nest" is another treehouse that our company built during the summer of 2001. Our challenge—as presented to us by the client—was to create something uniquely sexy and to spare no expense in the process. Needless to say, we had a great summer.* **OPPOSITE:** *The house is entirely suspended by seven Douglas fir trees. There is nearly as much deck space as there is finished interior space—about 600 square feet in all.*

ABOVE: It was decided that the property manager should have a treehouse of her own at the other end of the eighty-acre property.

OPPOSITE, TOP: It sure does not look like the office I work in, and this office is used every day.

OPPOSITE, BOTTOM: This poor fir tree is being asked to do a tremendous amount of work. So far, after three years, it appears to be in good health. Slowly, the tree will adjust to the new load it is carrying and add new wood where it is structurally appropriate.

OVERLEAF: Like all houses, a treehouse needs maintenance. In this case, we are keeping a close eye on all the tree connections to see how they fare in a very windy environment. After three years, we are observing that the second-growth firs are healthy and "putting on wood."

beams coming off the trees. From that point the perpendicular deck joist cantilevered over the beam another 4 feet. That effectively created a 10-foot-deep deck off the face of the trees, which, thanks in large part to the GLs, worked out very well.

The second treehouse, a structure containing 120 square feet of interior space and 100 square feet of outside decking, stands at the edge of a dense forest of second-growth fir and is supported by two larger Douglas firs that stand 14 feet apart and are about 24 inches in diameter. Three smaller firs were utilized to support the stairs and deck.

The summer we spent building Pam's treehouses will forever be a memorable one. Builder Shane Wyatt took the lead on the project, and over the course of four long months, he and four others cobbled together an exceptionally complicated and sprawling structure. Pam's project was one of the most ambitious we have completed to date.

ABOVE: *The deck overlooks a field and a man-made lake. Mount Rainier also looms large just off the left.*
OPPOSITE, TOP TO BOTTOM: *A whimsical winding staircase transports one up to the grand cottage in the trees. A beautifully carved wooden frog by artist Douglas McGregor, commissioned by the owner, stands guard in the vaulted living room. The cozy barrel-roofed bedroom looks back to the front door and north end of the living room. There is also a small, private bathroom just off one corner of the open bedroom.*

SYDNEY'S TREEHOUSE *Snoqualmie, Washington, U.S.A.*

There is a great book entitled *A Pattern Language* that was written back in the 1970s. In it the authors set forth many rules that architects should use when siting and designing a structure so that in the end it has that indescribable quality that convinces you that it works. One of the important messages from that book that has stuck with me over the years is a simple rule on siting a house on a larger piece of property. The rule states, one should go to whichever part of the given property that needs the most improvement and build there. In other words, do not go to the prettiest part of the property, as it is already beautiful and the chances of improving it would be unfavorable. At Sydney's place, we were trying to keep this in mind, but we just kept coming back to the most beautiful group of trees in the most beautiful setting. It happened to be the same place where Sydney's late husband Bill used to come to sit and enjoy nature.

Sydney had been dreaming of building a treehouse for quite some time. When her husband Bill was alive, they often talked about building one but it was one of those things that stayed low on the priority list. Now, she and her three beautiful daughters wanted to build a place to honor his memory.

Sydney teaches at our local elementary school and taught all three of my children. So when it was suggested by one of her colleagues that the community come together and help her build a treehouse, I jumped at the chance. It remains to this day one of my favorite treehouses.

Sydney was looking for a small room that she could fill up with mementos and cozy chairs for relaxing and reading. During the summer she offers reading classes to children, and this would be a place for that as well.

In 1999, Treehouse Workshop along with Sydney's family and friends finally built Sydney's Treehouse. With 115 square feet of interior space and 50 square feet of deck area, the treehouse was positioned about 14 feet off the ground. As with many of our other projects, we relied almost exclusively on reclaimed materials. For the beams, joists, and framing, we used reclaimed fir. The floors were done with salvaged oak flooring, the walls with cedar plank. The siding is 1' x 12' fir. Atop the roof is salvaged metal and a six-foot-long skylight.

ABOVE: *Sydney loves her treehouse and adorns it with many personal touches.* **OPPOSITE:** *The rustic cabin is perched in five trees at the top of a lushly forested hillside.*

TOP: *The views are of only the rainforest that the little house occupies.* **ABOVE:** *Moss grows everywhere, and the soft forest duff springs under your feet. The fresh aroma of rain and forest fills the nostrils and one knows instinctively that this is a special place.* **OPPOSITE:** *A simple stair takes one up between two main support trees—a cedar on the left, and a broadleaf maple on the right. All the materials used in the treehouse were, again, salvaged. Sydney found the windows, and we procured the rest. The railings came from the surrounding woods.*

ABOVE: *Without any previous experience, Sydney and her three daughters insulated and completely finished the interior of the treehouse.* **OPPOSITE, TOP:** *Obviously, they have an eye for decorating as well.* **OPPOSITE, BOTTOM:** *From the back. Positioning one's self a few yards further back, the treehouse disappears altogether.*

OUT 'N' ABOUT TREESORT *Cave Junction, Oregon, U.S.A.*

Every year at the Treehouse Conference, near Cave Junction, Oregon, we get to see at least one new Michael Garnier creation. He builds treehouses like I change my sheets, and then rents them out to an eager clientele. When we visited Michael for this book, we chose to photograph the Serendipitree (he plays on the word *tree* everywhere he can) treehouse, one of his more recent buildings. I think this building captures the essence of what treehouses are all about.

The Serendipitree is characterized by its rusticity—stair railings were fashioned from logs, the bark of which was laboriously removed by hand and then sanded to give it a smoothness to the touch. The same was done for the interior ladder.

ABOVE: *Here is what the top room looks like inside.*
OPPOSITE: *The "Tree Room Suite," Michael's fanciest treehouse, rents for $170 per night.*

ABOVE: *Inside one of Michael's 1997 creations, the Tree Room Suite. It's a beautifully appointed house in a network of small but strong white oaks.* **OPPOSITE:** *The master bedroom of the suite.*

TOP: *The Forestree treehouse from across the bridge.* **ABOVE:** *Many of Michael's single-tree treehouses employ this patent pending "Treezebo" platform system. From the GL's in the tree, a custom-fitted two-inch schedule-40 steel pipe extends outward as far as seven feet. The end of the pipe is picked up by a cable that is anchored higher in the tree to another set of GL's, thereby eliminating the need for knee braces below that platform.* **OPPOSITE:** *Another of Michael's recent creations, the Forestree, is far more challenging to get to. It's situated forty feet up in a fir tree, and you need to take a sixty-foot bridge to get there. (Not to mention the forty-foot climb up to the bridge.) Once there, many of the necessities of home—a sink and toilet—are within reach. The plumbing runs through the trunk.*

THE B'VILLE TREEHOUSE *Portland, Oregon, U.S.A.*

They grow big trees here in the Pacific Northwest, but when we were asked to come to this spot near Portland, Oregon, to plan a treehouse for a family here, I found a maple tree that put "big" to shame.

This gorgeous broadleaf maple has been growing for over a hundred years here on the sandy banks of the Willamette River, and it is now apart of the manicured grounds of an exceptional country estate. Seven separate trunks rise out of the same root system to create a base that is fifteen feet in diameter. It is a magnificent tree.

It took only a few minutes to sketch a fantasy house that fit naturally within the ring of the broadleaf maple's sturdy trunks. The only problem was that the client loved the drawing, which meant that we would then be charged with the daunting task of actually having to build it!

Four blissful months of creative carpentry and a lot of head-scratching later, we ended up with a wildly over-the-top children's treehouse that looked a lot like the sketch that it started from. It was a happy ending.

ABOVE: *Carver Douglas McGregor put his mark on another of our projects, this one for a family near Portland, Oregon, in the spring of 2000.* **OPPOSITE:** *This enormous broadleaf maple inspired a simple design that took an exceptionally long time to build. Never had we gone to such a high level of detail before, and only rarely have we gone there since.*

TOP: *The interior has antique wide-plank fir flooring, clear fir wall paneling, and a clear red cedar ceiling.*

ABOVE: *A found driftwood post anchors the spiral stairs that lead to the tower and second-story decks.*

OPPOSITE: *After the third month of construction, we had to remind ourselves that we are among the luckiest carpenters in the world.*

UPS AND DOWNS TREEHOUSE *Sonoma County, California, U.S.A.*

Andrew Fisher learned a lot while building his treehouse. When he began he had a certain design in mind, but what he designed was not what was ultimately built. The builder, Jonathan Fairoaks, did his best, but as every would-be treehouse builder comes to find out, the trees have the final say in how the treehouse will look. I think that the trees did a spectacular job.

But we must give credit where credit is due. Fisher makes his living as an interior designer, and as you can see, he is at the top of his game. He painted the faux-bois finishes himself and had all the walls upholstered in Lurex fabric, which literally glows in the candlelight. Imagine how wonderful this treehouse would feel during an evening gathering!

From the outside, all the carefully preserved branches are doing their best to obscure the rustic redwood siding. It is getting hard to see that the treehouse is there at all, in fact.

ABOVE: *It is getting hard to see the house through the trees, but once you arrive below the treehouse, you can instantly sense that something special is above.* **OPPOSITE:** *Something special in the air.*

OPPOSITE, TOP: *The front door is from India.* **OPPOSITE, MIDDLE:** *From the porch, there are excellent views of the Russian River.* **OPPOSITE, BOTTOM:** *Another beautiful door. This one was imported from China.* **ABOVE:** *As the redwood siding ages and the plants gain a foothold on the rope railings, the treehouse blends more and more into its surroundings.*

TOP: *The owner makes his living as an interior designer.* **MIDDLE:** *Windows are the most important part of a successful treehouse design. It is critical to take advantage of the vantage points.* **ABOVE:** *Stained glass adds a beautiful and colorful element that can broadcast throughout the space.* **RIGHT:** *Faux-bois finishes were applied to all the woodwork, and all the walls were upholstered in Lurex fabric, which literally glows in the candlelight.*

SARAH'S TREEHOUSE *Marin County, California, U.S.A.*

There are only a few other places in the United States where I could see our family living, and one would be somewhere along the northern coast of Central California. When, in the spring of 1998, my arborist friend, Jonathan Fairoaks, asked me to join him for a project in that very part of the United States, I jumped at the chance. He even let me bring along my oldest treehouse-building partner, John Mackenzie.

Sarah's treehouse is located near an assembly of small summer cottages and farms that cling to a north-facing slope overlooking Tomales Bay, about an hour and a half drive northwest of San Francisco. For the most part, the trees in this area grow on the north slopes and in the myriad creases and crevices of alluvial drainages. It was at the top of one such drainage where Sarah and her mother, Frederica, conscripted Fairoaks to build their treehouse.

The tree itself is a remarkably complicated Douglas fir. It appears that it has been repeatedly assaulted by Pacific storms, however, as its multiple trunks and branches shoot out in unusual ways. It is a majestic beauty nonetheless, and Fairoaks chose to take advantage of its enormous size by placing the treehouse's platform over forty feet up in the tree's cradling boughs.

The treehouse is used as a summer house for Sarah, while her mother lives full-time in a small house situated higher up the hill. What I remember most about building it is the severe weather that we endured while there. One day it rained so hard that my "waterproof" watch literally filled up with water. I also recall narrowly escaping a severe head-bonking when a saturated dead branch gave way 60 feet up in the tree. I heard the crack of it breaking and out of the corner of my eye caught a glimpse of an ominous black shadow descending from above. I was just starting to think about moving when a fifty-pound snag of wet wood brushed by my ear and stabbed into the soft ground at my feet. I hate when that happens.

It all turned out well in the long run, though. No one got hurt and I now have a place to stay in one of my favorite parts of the world.

ABOVE: *Not far from Ups and Downs is another Fairoaks creation that I had the pleasure of working on during the spring and fall of 1998. It stands forty-two feet up in the boughs on one of the most interesting old Douglas firs I have ever seen.*
OPPOSITE: *Jonathan Fairoaks had the platform nearly complete, and then called me in to design and build the house. Here I am six years later, back to take a photograph.*

OPPOSITE: *The treehouse serves as an overflow house for Frederica, her daughter Sarah, and husband, J.B. Not only is it high in the tree, but the tree is also high on a hill that overlooks narrow views of the Pacific Ocean.* **ABOVE:** *A Jonathan Fairoaks signature rope swing. He installs a doozy on every project and they are fun!*

TOP: *A look down from one of two opposing lofts that are tucked up in the eaves at each end of the house.* **ABOVE:** *In six short years a six-inch branch that was cut during construction has already healed over.*
OPPOSITE: *A cozy loft that gets regular use in the summer.*

BOY SCOUT TREEHOUSES *Monroe, Louisiana, U.S.A.*

Looking back at the many folks with whom we have collaborated to build treehouses, Dr. Ralph Armstrong of Monroe, Louisiana, has to be among the most persuasive clients we've had. I'll never forget the time he suggested he could have us picked up and brought to Monroe, in a private jet no less. As enticing as that sounded, it turned out that we were already scheduled to be on a project (one that I begged permission from my wife to be on) near New Orleans, so we would soon be conveniently close-by and could make the journey from there. When we informed Dr. Armstrong of this situation, he characteristically replied that he would simply have us flown in via the private jet from wherever we would be.

As we came to find out, Dr. Armstrong, or Dr. Ralph (as he is affectionately called around town), is an obstetrician. At last count, he had helped coax over 14,000 babies into this world. Naturally, upon meeting him I succumbed to his otherworldly powers and ended up tacking on another seven days to my trip. While doing so nearly cost me my marriage, I gained a family of lifelong friends.

Two summers later, we returned to the same fabulous Southern hospitality of Dr. Ralph's home to complete his vision of a complex of five interconnected treehouses at the Boy Scout camp in Monroe. With the help of talented bridge-builder Carroll Vogel and his Seattle, Washington-based company, Sahale LLC, the dream became a reality in Monroe. It was a wonderful collaboration.

ABOVE: *A metal bridge leads to one of the six treehouses built for a Boy Scout camp in Louisiana.*
OPPOSITE: *The Akaila Lodge was the first treehouse we built for the camp in the late winter of 1997.*

LEFT: *Two years later, we returned to build a series of five treehouses—all connected by bridges.*
TOP: *We have never been treated as well as we were by our hosts in Monroe, Dr. and Mrs. Ralph Armstrong. Their Southern hospitality made it an easy call when we were asked to return for the second phase of his treehouse dream.* **ABOVE:** *Spartan accommodations for the Boy Scouts.*

WELCH TREEHOUSE *Clinton, Mississippi, U.S.A.*

This neat Victorian-style treehouse for children has created quite a controversy in the city of Clinton, Mississippi. Last year, the Welch family fought and won a circuit court battle with the city of Clinton to keep their treehouse, which is located in the Welches front yard. But now the city is appealing that decision, taking it to the Mississippi State Supreme Court.

The problem seems to be that the treehouse was built in the front yard, when there are rules that forbid accessory buildings in front and side yards. Can we not make an exception and allow a "conditional use" here? Apparently not.

Despite overwhelming public support for the neighborhood treehouse, the city aldermen voted five to two to pursue this asinine appeal. It seems they are unable to see the treehouse through the trees.

Stay tuned to see what happens by checking on the Welches well-kept Web site at www.SaveOurTreehouse.com.

ABOVE: *The Welch family has been fighting to keep their treehouse for three years.*
OPPOSITE: *Harmless children's treehouses, or menacing nuisance? You decide.*

OPPOSITE: *It looks fun to me.* **TOP:** *A treehouse that clearly is dearly loved.* **ABOVE:** *And nicely decorated too!*

MILES'S TREEHOUSE *Long Island, New York, U.S.A.*

Visual artist Roderick Romero seems to always be working with a very interesting client, and this time it was the famous fashion designer Donna Karan. Romero and Karan go to the same yoga class in New York City, and it wasn't long before the talented designer of treehouses was whisked off to an estate on Long Island to begin sketching a concept for a treehouse for Karan's grandchild, Miles.

By this time, Romero and I had become friends, so when he called to see if I had time to lend a hand I could not refuse. Besides, I was born on Long Island and I love to visit there whenever I can.

Miles turned out to be one of our most excited and appreciative clients of all time, and Romero came through with a great design and some very funky building materials. I spent four days there with my building-project buddy, Ian Jones, getting the platform and walls constructed, before turning it over to Romero to finish. He did a nice job. I particularly like the copper roof and the wild ladder and railings.

ABOVE: *A diamond window centered in an antique door beckons you to Miles's treehouse in Long Island, New York. Our first collaboration with artist Roderick Romero turned out to be a tremendous amount of fun, and Miles was one of the most appreciative young clients we have ever had.* **OPPOSITE:** *Roderick did a great job in design and material acquisition. He found a variety of interesting old windows and some salvaged 1 x 8s, the likes of which I had never seen before.*

OPPOSITE, TOP: *Since this photo was taken, Roderick has gone back and installed a built-in Didgeridoo (the Australian outback instrument) that so captivated Miles and his younger brother, Mercer. One of Roderick's carpenters played one while we were working. After a lesson, Miles proved to be a natural at playing it.* **MIDDLE:** *The treehouse was commissioned by a famous designer, Donna Karan, for her grandchildren.* **OPPOSITE, BOTTOM:** *Salvaged and recycled materials were used wherever possible. This stair, as with all of the railings, was built with materials found on site.* **TOP:** *A beautiful walnut floor was stained darker to help the beautiful silver oak tree stand out even more.* **ABOVE:** *"Mushroom" wood siding has a great texture and look. Hopefully it can withstand the rigors of New York's weather.*

ALPHABET CITY TREEHOUSE *New York, New York, U.S.A.*

Twenty years ago, when Julie Kirkpatrick's son was born, she planted a willow tree in a vacant, burned out lot in Manhattan's then notoriously dangerous Alphabet City. It was at the beginning of a community movement to take back that part of town, which had been overridden by drug addicts and criminals. Now, that willow tree (wisely planted over an underground river) has grown big and strong, just like the movement to take back that part of the city.

Today the park is called "El Jardin Del Paraiso" (the garden of paradise), located at Fourth Street between Avenues C and D. Alphabet City, named for the simple alphabetized grid that names its streets, is now a thriving multi-ethnic success story.

Roderick Romero moved to Manhattan from Seattle a few years ago, and right away he pegged his neighborhood park's willow tree as a great place to build a treehouse.

ABOVE: *It took many months of campaigning and politicking but in the end Roderick prevailed and he was granted permission to build his simple treehouse dream. Roderick Romero in his tree.* **OPPOSITE:** *Children and adults alike are crazy about the treehouse. Just a seven-foot boost in elevation has boosted the spirits of the entire neighborhood.*

BIALSKI TREEHOUSE *Bridgehampton, New York, U.S.A.*

Technically, we are not dealing with a true treehouse here; it's more of a stilt house. This structure is so captivating, however, and it surely has the spirit of a treehouse, that it is worth presenting to you.

Bialski Treehouse is the work of Michael Ince, an artist and sculptor from Brookhaven, New York. Ince, who works out of his hobbitlike home and workshop on the edge of Long Island's Great South Bay, has a unique and beautiful style. He uses primarily a band saw to shape and sculpt large slabs of reclaimed fir and other odd bits of wood that he collects from all over the Northeast. He has been creating exceptional sculptures throughout his career, and I am sure it's only a matter of time before he is recognized as one of America's most talented contemporary artists.

The treehouse was built for property owner Jay Bialski's young children. There are so many wonderful details in the Bialski Treehouse that seeing it is sure to put a smile on your face.

ABOVE: *A Michael Ince treehouse sculpture on Long Island.* **OPPOSITE:** *Playful use of found woods, exaggerated swoops and sways, and carefully cut-out patterns combine to create a uniquely beautiful place to play.*

OPPOSITE: *Wisteria is quickly trying to obscure the artwork; I hope the owners keep it at bay.* **TOP**: *A short bridge to another world.* **ABOVE**: *Brilliant children's furnishings, also provided by the artist.*

ARMOUR TREEHOUSE *New Haven, Connecticut, U.S.A.*

After experiencing artist Michael Ince's intriguing work for the Bialski's in Bridgehampton, New York, we responded with an enthusiastic "let's go" when Ince suggested we drive to see another of his creations, a three-level treehouse in New Haven, Connecticut. Before we got on the road, though, he warned me that he wasn't quite finished with the structure. Actually, he said there was a chance that he may never finish it. Three hours later, standing on owner Gordy Armour's property and looking up at what Ince had made for the Armour family, I couldn't help but think otherwise; the treehouse was done.

ABOVE: *An enticing entry to another whimsical Michael Ince treehouse.* **OPPOSITE:** *Three levels of the treehouse are named after the Armour children: Robin's Nest, Charlottes Web, and Toby's Tower.*

ABOVE: *Michael's squid-like ridge decorations set his creation apart.* **TOP, LEFT TO RIGHT:** *The stairs make three complete revolutions around the tree to get up to Toby's Tower. A side room on the way up. The treehouse from behind.*

ROSS TREEHOUSE *West Falmouth, Massachusetts, U.S.A.*

Treehouses have a funny way of growing on you. Martha Ross is the mother of a great friend and fellow carpenter Nat Ross, who had lived in the Pacific Northwest for many years. Nat and I had many treehouse-building adventures together, and when his mother heard about what we were up to, she started to take an interest. It took me a few years to understand how keen her interest was. Eventually Martha sent us a letter from Massachusetts describing what she wanted. She said she wanted a treehouse, and she wanted it the next summer. In the letter she also wrote, "By the way, here is a deposit." Sometimes that is what it takes to get people like me moving. Actually, to be honest, I couldn't think of an easier job to get motivated for.

Along with being some of the nicest people I have ever met, Nat's parents live in one of the most beautiful places in the world. Their property sits at the head of a picturesque, white-sand harbor that is dotted with beguiling boats at anchor. It was arranged that I would arrive in September 2000 with two carpenters and that we would stay in the guesthouse on the property. Nat was already there, working on another project in the neighborhood. So if we were lucky, we might get to have him around as well.

Martha has a tight group of friends that golf and play cards together. The treehouse was to be a place for her to entertain her friends. From a more practical standpoint, it would also be a fun place to house "overflow" summer guests and her ever-growing family. Furthermore, it would be a garden folly that she could admire from the kitchen nook where she drinks her morning cup of coffee.

In keeping with the style of many of the summer cottages in the area, it was determined that the finished treehouse would have no insulation and that all of the framing would be visible. For that reason we chose to frame with remilled, old, tight-grained Douglas fir and similar 1" x 8" fir shiplap exterior sheathing. The floors were the same wide-plank fir, and the ceiling went right from fir 1" x 4" skip sheathing to western red cedar roofing shingles. The platform was constructed of massive reclaimed yellow pine beams and joists. Only two oaks were available to support the treehouse, so we harvested some 8- to 10-inch cedars from an adjacent property that was being developed and used them for posts. The windows and doors came all the way from Portland, Oregon, where two years before I had bought them from, of all people, Nat Ross!

Martha is a gardener, and she keeps the grounds of her classic Victorian waterfront home in impeccable condition. It is understated and overwhelmingly beautiful. The Ross Treehouse is just a few yards north of the main house on an empty lot that has grown over with sturdy oaks, thorny underbrush, and the occasional cedar. An ancient stone wall, about knee-high, separates it from Martha's gardens.

ABOVE: *A tranquil setting on the front deck of Martha's treehouse.* **OPPOSITE, TOP**: *We tried to pay homage to some of the great early Shingle Style homes that make up many of the houses in the area.*
OPPOSITE, BOTTOM: *A look from behind. Note the standard-issue treehouse electrical service: a yellow extension cord.*

ABOVE: *It is only a summer house, but I'm guessing the summer is at least a little more fun with a room such as this.*
OPPOSITE: *All the wall plates were framed extra low to keep the profile of the treehouse as low as possible. The roof line had to be lifted just to be able to walk out of the 6' 6"-tall door.*

FOREVER YOUNG TREEHOUSES *Burlington, Vermont, U.S.A.*

Bill Allen, an insurance salesman from Burlington, Vermont, called me about six years ago and asked what I thought about this wonderful vision he had of wheelchair-accessible treehouses. I can remember wanting to fly across the country the next day to give him a helping hand. Reality struck, however, and I stayed with my family in Fall City.

Three years later, Bill showed up at the Treehouse Conference in Oregon with pictures in hand. He had turned his vision into reality with two successful projects. Forever Young Treehouses, Inc. was a growing concern.

ABOVE: *James suffers from a neurological disorder that severely limits his ability to move and speak. The treehouse gives him a different experience.* **OPPOSITE:** *James's Treehouse in Milton, Vermont, was Bill Allen's first foray into the world of treehouse construction. Bill was director of the Make-A-Wish Foundation of Vermont, and it was a wish of James's to have a treehouse.*

LEFT: *Bill sought the advice of Yestermorrow Design/Build School in Warren, Vermont, where a team of students and teachers built this glorious experiment.* **ABOVE:** *In all, it is a very creative space, and I am sure it comes in handy for overflow guests at the school.*

There is something very seductive about this little house in the trees. Perhaps it is the beautiful curves of the side-wall shingles, or the forward-jutting entry. I have always loved a double pitch in a roofline.

TOP: *Here at Paul Newman's Hole in the Wall Gang Camp, in Ashford, Connecticut, an unexpected benefit of the 300-foot ramp that slowly rises through the trees is that many of the campers now have a chance to travel through and enjoy the woods.* **ABOVE:** *The prize that awaits them at the top is enough to make any kid squeal with joy.* **RIGHT:** *All the buildings at the Hole in the Wall Gang Camp are made to look like an 1880's Wild West town; the 600-square-foot treehouse is no exception. It was made to look like a hideout with its crooked doors, windows, and roof lines.*

OPPOSITE, TOP: *Just north of Burlington, in the town of Colchester, Vermont, a 120-foot ramp winds up through the oak and locus trees to an open 450-square-foot treehouse lodge that overlooks Lake Champlain. Cabinmates at Camp Ta-Kum-Ta now take turns sleeping overnight in a clubhouse that formerly was off-limits. "Treehouses have always been very exclusive clubs when you think about it," Mr. Allen explains. "Forever Young is trying to change all that."* **OPPOSITE, BOTTOM:** *Designed by James "B'fer" Roth, a rustic furniture builder and the chief builder and designer for Forever Young, the treehouse's interior radiates warmth.* **TOP:** *Good thing we took this shot when the leaves were off the trees.* **ABOVE:** *All ramps comply with the Americans with Disabilities Act, which requires a one-inch rise for each foot of ramp. This gradual climb gives the kids a chance to actually touch and feel the trees on the journey up to the treehouse.*

EWOK TREEHOUSE *Oxfordshire, England*

Treehouses are going through a major resurgence of interest in the United Kingdom at the moment. John Harris of The Treehouse Company in Scotland has been very busy creating custom treehouses like this one in Oxfordshire, England. His creative design staff modeled this after the famous Ewok village from the *Star Wars* installment *Return of the Jedi.*

At Ewok, what is already an almost surreal and somewhat spooky experience is magnified by the unsteadiness of the suspended ladder.

PRICE TREEHOUSE *Wales, United Kingdom*

For the longest time I was uncertain as to why I was building treehouses, but when I see a tree like this one in England, it reminds me that I found the answer. I build treehouses because I want to share in the energy of a strong, healthy tree. Ever since I can remember, when I got next to a big tree I automatically looked for ways to climb up into its branches. I wanted to be part of that tree, and the higher I could climb the better.

Nowadays, I just like to be around trees. After all, any thing that can stay in one place and get everything it needs to grow and be strong is amazing. There is nothing else in this world like a good tree. This is the real reason we all have been drawn to treehouses. It is the allure of the tree itself.

The Price family's treehouse in Wales is situated in a giant beech tree, a tree that has all the magnetism that I just described. Beech trees were everywhere where I grew up and for me they have always had a powerfully seductive quality. I love the smooth elephant-skin bark and the broad reach of its often low-level branches. It is a great climbing tree with characteristically striking proportions. It is not easy to build in a beech tree because it seems a crime to cut even one of its innumerable branches. Here, however, the Prices hit the nail on the head and blended their treehouse right into nature.

ABOVE: *A beautiful tree with a house to match, also built by The Treehouse Company.* **OPPOSITE:** *Mr. Harris claims to have built 500 treehouses over the last four years!*

GAINZA TREEHOUSE *Biarritz, France*

It would be difficult to determine which is the most obsessively designed treehouse, as most of the treehouses that I see are, well, obsessively put together. But the story of Gainza leads me to believe that we have a winner. Maxi Gainza Sr., an Argentine with roots in London, built his treehouse (two actually, but I will get to that later) on the property of his summer house Villa Bertha in the coastal city of Biarritz, France.

On the day we arrived to photograph the Gainza Treehouse, Maxi was not around. This was disappointing, as he sounds like a modern-day Renaissance man. Maxi is a pilot, a carpenter, a writer, and a highly successful businessman. He grew up in Argentina, but later moved to England to attend Oxford University. Along the way, he developed a passion for sailing.

Maxi's skills as a carpenter are considerable, and he is self-taught. He began the process of designing and constructing his treehouse just as most professionals would, by creating a scale model of his concept. Not long after completing the model, it was very enthusiastically received by his beloved Tango, his dog, who ate it in its entirety. Fortunately, by then the concept had been, for the most part, finalized. This treehouse, Maxi determined, would not be ordinary in any way. It would be a reflection of his passion for boating; it would be, well, a boat in a tree.

The cabin, perhaps the least complex part of the total structure in terms of assembly, was the first part to go into the tree. It went up in 1987. Several years passed before the main feature of the design, what the Gainzas call the "third floor," was erected in 1993. The process was anything but uneventful. "Dad was laying the keel when a storm hit and broke it," Maxi Jr. said. Some blood was shed, mostly on the band saw.

The hull design was copied from a sixteenth-century merchant ship. Working during the warm summer months and into October, Maxi had two other carpenters and four to five helpers on hand to construct it. The team set up a steam chest in the back of the boat, which they used to bend the wood that clads the hull. It was a hugely time-consuming process, as they could only steam two pieces at a time. Finally, in 1995, they completed work on the hull. A figurehead was soon added, a model of Maxi's daughter Zelmira.

ABOVE: *Maxi Gainza challenged his children to help build a faithful reproduction of an eighteenth-century sailing ship twenty feet up in a plane tree.* **OPPOSITE:** *A ship is an unlikely sight to see high in the trees of a beautiful French villa.*

Over a delicious lunch served to us in the garden of the Gainzas' property, Maxi's wife, Sasita, showed us photographs of another treehouse they had built—their first one. Like many first runs, it was often a frustrating learning experience. "It nearly drove us to divorce," Sasita declared. "I nearly broke my vocal cords calling for him to come down. He would come down for dinner at ten or eleven at night. It was awful, just awful. And he looked like a tramp! He ruined all of his clothes!" Ah, yes, I thought, this is a story I know very well.

ABOVE: *Maxi's daughter posed for the plaster figurehead.* **OPPOSITE, TOP:** *From further back, the ship almost disappears.* **OPPOSITE, BOTTOM:** *Looking aft.*

ABOVE: *The Captain's Quarters.* **OPPOSITE:** *The forward berth.*

LA CABANE PERCHÉE *Bonnieux, France*

Alain Laurens was bitten by the treehouse lovebug six years ago and has since pursued his passion with vigor. His use of extraordinarily fine materials, along with his eye for good design and his obvious pursuit of perfection, has put him at the top of the world of treehouse builders.

Alain built his experimental treehouse on the side of a hill in the boughs of a 100-year-old pine overlooking the dry and rocky foothills of Provence. It is the kind of place you would like to spend a month lounging by a pool while reading a good book and drinking chilled rosé with lunch. Unfortunately, our visit was strictly business, so while these other activities were being handily attended to by Alain's family, Radek and I made the scorching trek up to the treehouse to take pictures. We were both rejuvenated by what we saw. Despite the oppressive heat of the early-afternoon sun, Alain's treehouse doggedly cast its spell over us.

What catches the eye first is Alain's choice of woods—mostly teak and clear western red cedar. These are beautiful, often very expensive, woods to work with. Closer inspection reveals that this treehouse, unlike many out there, was not "thrown together." Each joint was expertly crafted to fit perfectly. (Even after six years the joints are still snug.) I also couldn't help but notice the attention given to avoiding any harm to the host. Steel brackets with tough rubber backing are strung together in a network around the tree with heavy "all-thread," which makes it possible to adjust the tension as the tree grows. All of the connections are adjustable, including the knee braces. There are no penetrations in the tree.

Everything about La Cabane Perchée seemed to be carefully planned, and I have to say that this is a great example of how to go about significant treehouse building without making any host-tree penetrations. Pines such as this one can be very sensitive trees, and in this arid climate they will grow rather slowly. Alain's construction may be the best solution for this climatic situation.

Climbing the stairs through a hatch, visitors of La Cabane Perchée are quickly immersed in a world of honey- and chocolate-colored brass and wood fittings. An assortment of earth-toned hats hang on one wall above the carefully concealed solar power controls. Beautiful horsehair paintbrushes hang in the cavities of cedar-stud walls. There is a well-padded bench that folds down from a wall once the entry hatch is closed, and on the oppo-

ABOVE: *Shade is critical in this part of Southern France.* **OPPOSITE:** *It was a pleasure to see beautiful western red cedar (wood from my part of the world) used with such care and integrity so far from home.*

TOP: *The skill and effort in design and execution was enough to take one's breath away.* **ABOVE:** *The tiny house had more interesting details than a nice house ten times larger.* **OPPOSITE:** *If Radek and I didn't need to push on, I would have spent a month here.*

site wall is a small writing desk. Here and there are miniature wood boxes, a bird cage, decorative fans, and other objets d'art. It is seductive and sumptuous, a room that succeeds shamelessly in its effort to soothe and calm the soul. The world would be a better place if Alain were its decorator!

Stepping onto the deck, one is greeted with more intricate woodwork details and a spectacular view of hills rolling down past a nearby farmhouse and across the valleys and the chalky canyons and cliffs of the beautiful foothills of southeastern France. The crazy tree limbs of the old pine reach up through the middle of the deck and create a broad and bristly canopy directly overhead. The place is hard to beat.

CHÊNE-CHAPELLE *Allouville, France*

The Chêne-Chapelle, a chapel in an oak, in Allouville, France, was far more than I had ever expected. The care that the people of Allouville have taken to keep this ancient oak alive and upright is extraordinary. The structure itself is equally spellbinding. I had heard about this church in the trees for many years, so when it came time to point our car in the right direction and actually find it, it was like a long-distance treasure hunt.

The church's caretakers are meticulous about keeping the grounds of Chêne-Chapelle looking beautiful.

TOP: *The upper chapel is reached by a spiral staircase that wraps around the outside of the 800-year-old oak.*
ABOVE: *The lower chapel is slightly larger but nonetheless quite cramped.* **OPPOSITE:** *The trunk of the great oak has been meticulously protected on the outside with thousands of tiny oak shingles. The hollow core of the ancient oak was reinforced at great expense with an intricate framework of welded steel pipe.*

ROBINSON TREEHOUSES *Paris, France*

For well over half a century, starting in 1848, the hip place to go outside of Paris on the weekends was the town of Robinson. Joseph Gueusquin started a trend by building a small restaurant in the boughs of one of the area's enormous chestnut trees. Word spread and people started to make the eight-mile pilgrimage from Paris. Soon, other entrepreneurs began opening their own treehouse restaurants. At the height of its popularity, there were ten such restaurants and countless other treehouse attractions. The popularity of treehouses seems to have been brought on by the publication of *Swiss Family Robinson* by Johann David Wyss in 1812–13. The town even changed its name to promote their attractions. Upon visiting the little town of Robinson last summer, I had the eerie but thrillingly exciting chance discovery of one of the famous trees. Hidden in the courtyard of a modern apartment complex, I was drawn to a spot where the last vestiges of the magnificent tree show that it is still barely clinging to life.

ABOVE: *This print was given to me by Robinson's librarian. What a wonderful place this must have been.*
OPPOSITE: *"Vrai Arbre," or "Real Tree," shown here in a lithograph, was one of the early and most popular treehouses in Robinson. The post on the left still props up one of the chestnut's great branches, but the tree today is chopped and broken and displays little evidence of its former glory.*

DANCING LIME TREEHOUSE *Peesten, Germany*

The Germans have known how to enjoy themselves for a long time, and if any one thing can prove that, their Dancing Lime Treehouse will. Built around 1760, the treehouse's beautiful stone staircase winds twelve feet up to an oak timber–framed platform that surrounds a plane tree. It is used on special occasions for playing music, dancing, and drinking. There are several examples of these whimsical structures throughout Germany, but this one in Peesten has been kept up the best. In fact, in the late 1990s an entirely new timber frame was constructed, and the site's lime tree (this one planted in the 1950s) is only now beginning to get its branches trained to fill in around the open windows.

If you've never been to Dancing Lime, it can be challenging to find, as the treehouse is somewhat disguised by the formality of these columns and stairway.

UPPER LEFT: *Inside the bower there is ample room for as many as 200 revelers, and a band as well. In the winter, the floorboards are removed and stored in a shed next door.*
BOTTOM LEFT: *This drawing shows the Peesten treehouse in the 1800s. It was built by a nobleman in order to entertain his hunting buddies while they were staying in his opulent stone lodge, which is still directly across the street.* **ABOVE:** *The tree is starting to fill out nicely.*

CASA DEL SOLE DI MEZZANOTTE *Tuscany, Italy*

I still hold out hope that Neil Young or Bruce Springsteen will someday call me to build a treehouse. In the meantime, I was able to live vicariously through Roderick Romero, who succeeded in lining up a gig with a rock star. In the summer of 2001, Romero was hired to build a treehouse on Sting's estate in Tuscany. Some people have all the luck!

Actually, luck didn't have much to do with it. For years, Romero was the lead singer and songwriter of the successful Seattle-based band Sky Cries Mary. It was during this time that he got to know the rock and roll icon. Actually, Sting's wife, Trudie Styler, had heard stories of Romero's dabbling in treehouses, and it was she who asked him to come up with a proposal for a treehouse that would be built near their summer house in Italy. After a brief site visit in late winter, Romero and his building partner, Wolfgang, returned to Tuscany the next summer to create this extraordinary building.

Apparently Sting has a fascination with ancient Druid culture, so Romero incorporated aspects of it into the design of the treehouse. In researching the subject, Romero learned that oak trees play an important role, and circular forms are very important.

Many other details found their way into Sting's treehouse, including bells and wind chimes (the Druids are said to have favored them), and a beautiful stained-glass window that represents the three suns of Druid folklore: blue for morning, yellow for mid-day, and red for sunset.

Armed with this kind of insight, Romero found the perfect oak tree, far from the main house and at the edge of a small lake. It was there that he and Wolfgang spent three months building and toiling during a hot Tuscan summer.

The treehouse is about 150 square feet big and octagonal in shape. It has live edge oak and copper siding and a meticulously constructed copper roof. There is another 120 square feet of outdoor deck space that comes to a point 35 feet over the lake. When Sting arrived, sight unseen, for the grand opening celebration, he was blown away. They say he stood speechless for a while, smiling ear to ear, before Romero heard him say, "Very inspiring." I would agree.

ABOVE: *Sting finds his treehouse to be "very inspiring." At one end of the treehouse, the railing comes to a point over the lake like the prow of a ship.* **OPPOSITE**: *"It goes from earth to stone to air," explains the builder. One enters the octagonal structure through a matching octagonal porthole in the floor.*

ABOVE: *The treehouse is twenty feet off the ground but thirty-five feet off the lake.* **OPPOSITE, TOP:** *The framing material was milled from trees that came down in storms on the property. The entire estate, in fact, strives to be 100% self-sufficient.* **OPPOSITE, BOTTOM:** *The floor is oak that is pigmented blue on the compass points. Posts rise up from the floor to support the roof.*

BERGMANN'S TREEHOUSES *Görlitz, Germany*

There is a place in easternmost Germany—as far east as you can go without going into Poland—that is the most fantastic exhibit of one man's passion for building that I have ever seen. Juergen Bergmann, the owner and craftsman of the property, has spent the last fifteen years creating this playground, among other fascinating things, that would have made Walt Disney jealous. Bergmann lives here, too, and he uses his home as a laboratory for testing his creative ideas.

Today, he is known throughout much of Europe for his beautifully detailed carved-log and natural-wood playground structures, all of which are on display at his place near Görlitz. Bergmann's place has become a mecca for active families of the area. Each of the structures he has created, as you'll see in the photos, is one of a kind and masterfully constructed. Of course, we are here to see his main treehouse, but it soon becomes clear that a few fun distractions stand between us and Bergmann's Treehouses.

Underground, beneath all of Bergmann's wood creations, are more than 500 yards of underground tunnels. Following Bergmann's directions to enter, we soon find that many sections of the tunnel system are devoid of light and are quite narrow. Being a tall guy and a little claustrophobic, I often find myself in a minor panic down there, but it seems that whenever I turn to flee back from whence I came, Bergmann is there to block my retreat. Pride turns me around again, and I push through to the light. It is exhilarating.

On the far end of the compound, Bergmann built a Kremlin-like castle/funhouse. He leads me up a stair to the top of it and into one of the structure's onion domes. Getting up there is nothing compared with getting back: the castle has a slide that drops visitors on their way out rather drastically into a dark dungeon-like space. It is a serious challenge to find your way out. I hadn't felt so alive in a long time!

It was 100 degrees that day, so instead of pushing on—we'd been touring Bergmann's for three hours and still hadn't seen the treehouse, mind you—Bergmann suggests that it would be a good idea to take a swim. We hop into his wildly painted Volkswagen van and drive down the back forty of his property to the Neisse River, the small river that separates Germany from Poland. Getting into the cool water just below a small set of rapids, we swim across to the other side. It is my first time in Poland. Now I can say that I have been there and I was naked the entire time.

ABOVE: *Many of Juergen's structures are experimental. This duck house actually breaks down so it can be transported to exhibitions in other places.* **OPPOSITE:** *A challenge course of zip lines threads through one end of the park. I didn't see anyone try it.*

Back at his property, Bergmann continues to play me like a fiddle. In fact, it is only after dinner that he suggests we have a little wine up in the treehouse. First, however, we have to get there from his house. The Bergmann house is a uniquely reinvented four-story barn. An elaborate elevated walkway—a network of half-timbers that are suspended by cables 25 feet off the ground (thankfully, there are railings)—connects the house to two treehouses. As we head toward the main treehouse, we encounter the other, the one called One Day Treehouse. The first treehouse built on the property, One Day was Bergmann's creation for his kids, though he says they rarely use it. It's a fun treehouse, and even has a bed.

One Day Treehouse is actually a Volkswagen van positioned in the top of a chestnut tree. We quickly discover that it is a little tricky to get into. Only after climbing over the roof of Bergmann's house and onto to a small deck, and then descending from the deck, do we get into the Volkswagen in the chestnut tree.

After a few more turns, the main treehouse comes into view. Situated high above all of Bergmann's other fantastic creations is one great treehouse, beckoning us, as it were, from its ancient oak host. Finally, we are there; the time has come to enjoy a little wine and view the treehouse up close.

ABOVE: *There was a new adventure around every corner. Many of them caused my claustrophobic tendencies to kick into high gear.* **OPPOSITE:** *The tree that supports this house is actually the large trunk of an oak tree that was de-barked, sanded, and then turned upside down. The roof is made of tired rubber conveyor belts that served the area's major coal industry; the wire cages are strong, stainless steel, human-scale habitrails.*

ABOVE: *Juergen has a penchant for putting things up in trees.* **OPPOSITE, TOP**: *Twenty feet above Juergen's driveway is a bridge that leads to a wacky, open stairway that takes one ten feet higher to a long ramp. The ramp eventually leads to the front door of Juergen's brilliant treehouse. The treehouse is in the top of this magnificent oak tree, which is actually rooted on a lower-level field, one that is another thirty feet below Juergen's driveway. (It's a little complicated to describe, but it's great.) That puts the treehouse at an elevation of at least sixty feet off the ground. It feels like it's 160 feet off the ground!* **OPPOSITE, BOTTOM LEFT**: *Inside, Juergen's treehouse feels like a seventeenth-century sailing ship, replete with artifacts like the gimbaled candle holder on top of the writing desk. We stayed up much too late in there on the night we visited.* **OPPOSITE, BOTTOM RIGHT**: *The treehouse has a second means of ascent.*

TATRY TREEHOUSE *Zakopane, Poland*

Before we left Germany, Juergen told us of a treehouse some five hours to the southeast, in the Polish town of Zakopane. We learned that the majority of homes in Zakopane are of log construction—most built the old-fashioned way. The churches here, several of which are at least a few hundred years old, are also mostly timber. Everything in Zakopane is made by hand, and there are many highly skilled carpenters living in the region. With this in mind, it seemed natural that there would be at least one neat treehouse there. So, onward we went.

Zakopane, a town whose history goes back a little more than four centuries (a young town relative to many other cities in Poland), is about an eight-hour drive from Warsaw and is situated in the most picturesque region in Poland. Besides being a major ski-resort town (its stunning Tatra Mountains were in consideration for the host site of the 2006 Winter Olympics), Zakopane is also known for its relation to Pope John II, who lived near here as a child and has returned here ceremoniously many times. The locals, called highlanders, are very loyal to the preservation of their rich folk heritage and are some of the friendliest people we met on our journey.

It is not uncommon for Zakopane to receive four to five feet of snow during the winter months, so any treehouse, or house for that matter, must be designed and built to sustain heavy snowfall. Most importantly, if a treehouse is to be enjoyed here during the winter, it must have a very efficient source of heat. Otherwise, better to designate it a treehouse for use during the very mild temperatures of the summer months, which is what the owners of Tatry Treehouse chose to do when designing it.

We arrived in Zakopane just after a considerable snowfall, so we didn't get to spend any quality time in the little blond treehouse. Still, we were glad we took Juergen's advice to visit here. With its smooth timber limbs (the tree bark is hand-peeled, then each limb is sanded) and interesting sculptural quality, Tatry Treehouse turned out to be a great find.

One might say that Tatry Treehouse is designed in the Zakopianskie style of wood architecture that originated here and characterizes most of Zakopane's houses.

ABOVE AND OPPOSITE: *Each piece is smoothed and sanded. It must feel great to climb on. Zakopane has a population of 33,000 full-time residents, the majority of whom can trace their family background to the town's original settlers of the 1500s. Radek found the local language to be quite different from the modern Polish that is spoken in his home city of Szcecin, which is located at the opposite end of the country, near the Baltic Sea. In Zakopane, locals speak a language that is a combination of Hungarian, Slovakian, and old and modern Polish. Fortunately for us, "treehouse" was a recognized word.*

KOROWAI TREEHOUSE *Irian Jaya, Indonesia*

The Korowai people of Irian Jaya, Papua New Guinea, actually live in treehouses. When an article came out in *National Geographic* a few years ago about this amazing culture, I promised that I would visit one day. The logistics became overwhelming, however, so I contacted the photographer who took the photos. As it turns out, there was quite an adventure in getting these photos to begin with. Photographer G. Steinmetz feels he was lucky to return from Papua New Guinea with his life! It may seem like a simple life high in the trees. Unfortunately, it is anything but. Tribes in the area are constantly warring, and one of the main reasons they choose to live in the trees is for self-protection.

Korowai is a fine example of what architect Frank Lloyd Wright called Organic Architecture—a building perfectly in harmony with its site. The poles, taken from the surrounding forest, are held together by rattan—also taken from the immediate surroundings.

ABOVE: *Once the poles have been fastened with the rattan rope, the treehouse's roof is covered with Sago palm leaves.*
OPPOSITE: *The treehouse is home to three brothers. Hopefully none of them snores at night!*

RIKARDS FAMILY TREEHOUSE *Nelson, New Zealand*

With a population of about 40,000, the nature-lovers city that is Nelson is a great place to build a treehouse. In this part of New Zealand, where one cannot travel far without arriving at a farm or orchard, forestry is among the primary industries, so materials are never in short supply. Nelson is also known for its fantastic crafts and locally made wines and beers, so we had much to be excited about as we headed toward the northwestern half of the top of the South Island, where Nelson is located.

After visiting the beautiful Abel Tasman National Park, Kahurangi National Park, and Nelson Lakes National Park, each located in the city of Nelson, it was time to seek out the treehouse. We were told of a modest-looking structure, a simple treehouse attached to a tree that had long since passed. Driving toward the site, from a considerable distance we could see the owner's little red cottage, its corrugated metal roof and clapboards evidently a sign of the local building vernacular. Adjacent to the house by a few dozen feet is the treehouse. Raised from the ground only about five feet, Nelson Treehouse is quite modest, at least at first glance. It is a do-it-yourselfer, the kind of treehouse one might encounter in backyards of homes anywhere in the world, really. Made of odds and ends—plywood, two-by-fours, and other recycled materials—it isn't exactly extraordinary in terms of its craftsmanship or materials. What is interesting about it, Radek suggested, is its shape, which bears a resemblance to the Deconstructivism-style house designed and built by world-renowned architect Frank O. Gehry in Santa Monica, California.

Treehouses can be constructed of a variety of found materials—odds and ends. If the tree is strong and the materials are attached appropriately, a modest-looking structure such as this can be around for years of enjoyment.

FUR 'N' FEATHERS RAINFOREST TREEHOUSES *North Queensland, Australia*

Australia, Queensland especially, is home to many treehouses, so deciding on one was not an easy thing. Fur 'n' Feathers, a treehouse eco-resort, happens to be sited in an amazing location, right in the middle of a rainforest. Here in the mountains behind the city of Cairns, reside treehouse-lovers such as the Brushtail Possum, the Pademelon Wallaby, and a variety of rare and endangered species, including the Cassowary, the Green Possum, and the Tree Kangaroo. That some of these little guys tend to climb trees for a living means that each treehouse's doors and windows have to be carefully designed and built to ensure a certain level of security. No need to worry about four-legged visitors popping in, however. Fur 'n' Feathers has gone out of its way to befriend these locals and does a reliable job of keeping them out of the Jacuzzi. Just remember to bring along a pair of binoculars, a camera, and a trusty birdwatching guidebook, as there is much to see.

ABOVE: *An inviting bedroom high in the rainforest of Queensland, Australia.* **OPPOSITE:** *This particular treehouse at Fur 'n' Feathers overlooks a river, making it possible for the truly adventurous to partake in a little fishing, right from the deck.*

Being a hotel, Fur 'n' Feathers is outfitted with many of the conveniences of the typical modern home. Its spacious deck comes equipped with a BBQ.

This rental treehouse came about through an economic exchange program with Sanya City in China and its sister city in Maui, Hawaii. It was the brainchild of David Greenberg, an architect on the island of Maui, who runs a treehouse bed-and-breakfast back in his home state. Greenberg claims to have tapped into a gold mine, and the local government in China wants to help him build many more. The treehouse has a hand-built look that fits nicely into the gnarly limbs of the tree. It even has a great view out toward the South China Sea.

ABOVE: *An organic spiral stair winds up a knarled tamarind tree on the coast of the South China Sea.*
OPPOSITE: *The lower level is suspended on posts, while the upper level is cradled by the tree's branches.*

ABOVE AND OPPOSITE, TOP: *The building inspectors in the United States may not like this railing, but I do.*
OPPOSITE, MIDDLE: *A cozy bedroom with a ladder that leads up to a sleeping loft.*
OPPOSITE, BOTTOM: *The bedroom peers out over the treetops to the sea.*

HALE TREEHOUSE *Hainan Province, China*

A most remarkable treehouse is sited not far from another of David Greenberg's treehouse creations in China. It is a traditional Hawaiian hale, built as part of the same economic exchange that brought Greenberg to the other site just down the road.

Everything about this beautiful little building radiates Polynesia. It was built by Francis Sineci, who is rapidly becoming famous for building faithful recreations of traditional Hawaiian-style houses (called hales) using time-honored methods of construction. The further one looks into the photographs of Hale Treehouse, the more beautiful this house seems.

Stilt houses like this one are still plentiful in the South Pacific. It is a practical structure for the environment, and if surrounding trees lay out properly, how could there be a better post system? In this case, Sineci used the native Eucalyptus trees to his advantage and posted up right off of them. Hale Treehouse is essentially a two-story house with no walls. I'm sure my local structural engineer would say that a house like this shouldn't stand given that it doesn't have any walls to give it shear strength. But maybe that is part of what makes it magic?

ABOVE: *This traditional Hawaiian hale treehouse is in China. It was built by Frances Sineci and was part of the same economic exchange that David Greenberg had participated in with the treehouse on page 174.* **OPPOSITE:** *The treehouse was designed to allow air to flow unobstructed.*

ABOVE: *Eucalyptus trees act as the posts to hold this otherwise very traditional hale in the air.* **OPPOSITE:** *Building off the ground was necessary in order to escape coastal floods from typhoons and the occasional tsunami.*

TSUYOSHI'S TREEHOUSE *Ise-Shima National Park, Japan*

There is no doubt that my first treehouse book struck a nerve in the United States when it came out in 1994. It was not long before Japan started to show an interest. In 1996, an outdoor magazine in Japan organized my first overseas project. I was thrilled and amazed that this simple carpenter (I got to bring my wife and best carpenter buddy too) was being flown to Tokyo to lead a job in the mountains two hours north of the city.

It was there that I met Takashi Kobayashi, a man with a passion for treehouses, among many other things, and we have been friends ever since. Each year "Taka" comes to the Treehouse Conference in Oregon and brings at least six to eight friends from home. When I told him it was my turn to visit Japan last summer, he rolled out the red carpet. We spent over a week together traveling all over Japan to visit all of the projects that he knew about. I could not have had a better host. "Kampai!"

ABOVE: *Two of my friendly tour guides, Tsuyoshi and Naoki, peeking out from a creation they built the summer before my arrival.*
OPPOSITE: *Building materials in Japan are not that much different from those in the United States.*
OVERLEAF: *The treehouse is used for entertainment as part of a campground.*

つり橋(suspension bridge)
定員　2person Only
フロントにお問合せ下さい。

OPPOSITE, TOP: *In the Japanese Shinto way of thinking, all natural things have a god within them. Therefore, it is very hard for the people to accept putting a nail or a bolt into a tree. The method of "sandwiching" the trunk or limbs with wood blocks I cannot recommend, as these connections easily slip and can otherwise cause far more stress for the tree than a simple bolt.* **OPPOSITE, BOTTOM:** *As treehouses become more and more popular in Japan, I hope to be able to demonstrate that a well-placed bolt will not hurt the tree.* **TOP:** *The treehouse overlooks a finger of salt water.* **ABOVE:** *Everything, including the windows, was built on-site.*

GEN'S TREEHOUSE *Nagano, Japan*

Dramatically situated about 8½ miles up a steep and winding mountain road and through a forest of small trees and large boulders, Gen's Treehouse is in an area that is far enough south that it rains frequently, almost exclusively during the winter months. On the day of our trek in, luckily there was mist in the air, enough precipitation to at least partially obscure our view of the hair-raising drops that threatened us only a few feet away on the starboard side of the road. Once parked, we hiked about a half mile to where Gen was waiting for us with a team of once-a-month treehouse builders, each a volunteer. The devoted group has been meeting like this for almost two years, with only an occasional missed meeting here and there. They greeted us with great enthusiasm and then led us in the direction of the site.

Gen is a research diver and runs the local dive shop here. One-half of his treehouse-building team was made up of friends from the dive shop, while the others came from an advertisement that Gen placed in the local newspaper, announcing a volunteer treehouse-building workshop.

The planning of the treehouse started in January 2000, with the first order of business being the selection of the tree. The group settled on a large fir—wood considered by loggers to be too weak for furniture, so usually left to continue in its growth. With cedar peeler poles and spruce as their primary structural materials, Gen and company designed and built a single-room, cedar-shake-roofed structure with a deck, which is accessed via a rigid bridge.

Seeing the treehouse in person for the first time, I was struck by how much it reminded me of the one featured in Kenneth Brower's 1978 book *The Starship and the Canoe*. Gen's is an inspired design.

ABOVE: *A simple treehouse rises up through the mist.* **OPPOSITE, TOP:** *It was hard to get a good look at it.*
OPPOSITE, BOTTOM: *Gen stands proudly next to his humble creation.*

TOP: *Stick railings are a common thread in treehouse designs around the world.* **BOTTOM**: *A sunburst of stained glass brightens up the tiny structure.* **OPPOSITE**: *My friend Hiroshi finds it funny that I would be balancing on such a small branch, thirty feet up in the air.*

SCULPTURE TREEHOUSE *Tokamachi City, Japan*

The village where this treehouse is located is called Tokamachi City, and I would guess that there are no more than 200 souls that live there. The town sits high at the end of a road at the end of a valley. It is anchored by an ancient Shinto shrine that is surrounded by majestic cedar, Kayaki, and beech trees.

Our tour rolled into town at just the right time. Takahide Mizuuchi, the young artist who organized and designed the treehouse, was presenting his finished product to the village that very evening. After the townsfolk completed the happy tour of the new treehouse, a celebration ensued at the community center. Much sake was had by all.

ABOVE: *The Japanese treehouse gang.* **OPPOSITE:** *A look down at the treehouse from thirty feet up a Kayaki tree.*

OPPOSITE, TOP: *A look back at the house from out on a limb. The interior was painted black in the tradition of Japanese teahouses and places of meditation. The black walls do not compete for light among the dazzling green foliage of the surrounding trees.* **OPPOSITE, BOTTOM:** *The door slides into the wall and disappears.* **TOP:** *A simple table and stool were added just before the celebration.* **MIDDLE:** *Wonderful old beams supplied by one of the villagers were used to support the decking.* **ABOVE:** *The open end of the treehouse is deceptively high off the ground. The treehouse is practically built on a cliff.*

TAKA'S TREEHOUSE AND TREEHOUSE BAR *Tokyo, Japan*

While in Japan, I learned that Japanese culture is very regimented. Everyone seems to be pointed in the same direction, and as a result, many amazing things get accomplished. Just driving through this mountainous country and witnessing the lengths they have gone to in order to make road travel safe and efficient is mind-boggling. We traveled through perhaps 100 tunnels, and one was seven miles long! Yet, underneath this dedicated and hard-working society, the youth culture is trying to express its individuality. My host, Taka, is a leader in this move-ment. He is clearly endowed with all the work ethics of his culture and deeply respects the Japanese Shinto phi-losophy, but he constantly tries to open people's eyes to self-expression. His treehouses give him the chance to do that in a delightfully pointed way.

ABOVE: *Many volunteers came together to make this little treehouse happen in downtown Tokyo.* **OPPOSITE:** *It is like an oasis in a land of brick and concrete.*

ABOVE, LEFT: *The way up.* **ABOVE, RIGHT:** *The colored windows pay homage to the reggae culture that is synonymous with the treehouse segment of Taka's crowd.* **OPPOSITE, TOP:** *Taka's treehouse bar, Café Au Go Go, in a trendy part of downtown Tokyo.* **OPPOSITE, BOTTOM:** *The little treehouse surrounded by high-rise buildings and asphalt.*

OPPOSITE: *Looking back from the treehouse to the bar at Café Au Go Go.* **TOP:** *Cozy place.* **ABOVE:** *No shoes are allowed in this section of the treehouse.*

TREEHOUSE CONCEPTS TREEHOUSE *Maui, Hawaii, U.S.A.*

This precise little treehouse is well off the beaten path up in the hills of the island of Maui. It was built by a fellow treehouse builder, Kama Lei Cook, for use as a show house for his fledgling business, Treehouse Concepts of Maui. He also lives here. Kama used all the latest support technology that he learned of while attending the Treehouse Conference in Oregon a few years ago. It looks like it is right out of *Sunset* magazine! Treehouses have been popular for many years in Hawaii, so I would imagine that Kama will stay very busy. He did a beautiful job on his own treehouse.

Kama built a very concise structure, one that has a certain retro look to it.

ABOVE: *Kama is making use of all the latest technology to keep this treehouse in the trees.* **OPPOSITE, TOP:** *Kama's dog living on island time.* **OPPOSITE, BOTTOM:** *Wainscoting is a great way to break up a wall and give a treehouse a touch of class.*

ISLAND WOOD TREEHOUSE *Bainbridge Island, Washington, U.S.A.*

Island Wood is an environmental learning center that is situated on approximately 250 wooded acres on the south end of Bainbridge Island, near Seattle, Washington. The property, like so many in the area, was thoroughly logged—but that was many years ago and now the second growth has matured into a beautiful forest. The trees here are a mix of Douglas fir, broadleaf maple, hemlock, and western red cedar. The forest floor is carpeted with native fern and salal. Most impressive of all, though, is Island Wood's host tree—a majestic Douglas fir that stands in a small clearing that overlooks a two-acre bog.

The treehouse is the work of a collaboration between builders Treehouse Workshop, Inc., working with Dale West and Les Laforge, and the office of Mithun Architects of Seattle. As with so many treehouse projects, Island Wood was made with salvaged and recycled materials throughout. The only "new" materials used are the split shakes of the exterior cladding. Everything about this project was big, so the timbers used in support of both the platform and the walls were sized accordingly. The main support beams in this "umbrella style" platform are 4" x 8" Douglas fir, and the knee braces are 4 x 6. The flooring consists of massive 3" x 12" remilled lumber with a tongue and groove so it could span the long distance (as far as six feet) between the beams. The walls were constructed in a timber-frame, post-and-beam style. Salvaged 3" x 8" fir from an old building in Seattle makes up the corner post and roof rafters. Also salvaged and remilled is fir tongue-and-groove flooring, which was done to create the skip sheathing on the exterior walls and roof. At this site there are occasionally heavy winds, so the stair system was designed with this in mind. It is gimballed with a heavy steel bracket at the main level; at the base it is free to "travel" on thick plastic skids. Because of the mild winters here, there is no need for insulation.

The owners wanted a treehouse that could serve as a classroom, capable of accommodating as many as fourteen students and a teacher. They also wanted it to overlook the bog, so that criteria guided what became a lengthy design process. It took several years, in fact, as the first two locations were deemed unacceptable by an arborist, who determined that laminated root rot was prevalent in many of the hemlocks on the property, making them prone to blow down in heavy winds. Then the great Douglas fir was found. Estimated to be 150 years old, it is 42 inches

ABOVE: *A grand staircase leads up to this extraordinary classroom in a tree.* **OPPOSITE**: *A look at the classroom tree-house from across the bog. A rain hat at the peak and a handcrafted wrought-iron railing at the doors has been added since this photo was taken.*

LEFT: *From below, the treehouse looks like a wood space capsule.* **TOP:** *The initial design program called for absolutely no glass in the treehouse, as that would make it an easy target for vandals. So, Dale built some beautiful shutters with purple heart and oak dowel latches.* **BOTTOM:** *Engineer Charlie Greenwood specially designed some GL's to receive the bottoms of the knee braces.*

ABOVE: *A walk along the nature trail reveals this glimpse of the treehouse from across the bog.* **OPPOSITE:** *One way to cover the gap between the floor decking and the tree is to use curving driftwood. At seventeen feet off the ground, the huge fir is still over three feet thick.*

thick at breast height and is growing at a rate of ten growth rings per inch. (With this growth rate in mind, all the structural hardware was created to allow for fifty years of growth. The hardware can also be retrofitted if need be.)

The treehouse was to be 230 square feet. The basic program, or guiding purpose of the design, had students grouped on the bog side of the tree with massive doors that would open and reveal the natural beauty of the bog and the surrounding forest. From this perspective, the students would be able to see how the bog is formed and the concentric rings created through its life cycle. It was important to the owner that no windows be incorporated into the design, so shutters and several skylights were utilized instead.

Because the treehouse was to be built in a public-private setting, Treehouse Workshop was charged with getting a permit for its construction, which in many places can be difficult to obtain since building codes for treehouses don't exist. As luck would have it, the lead inspector on the island was said to have lived in a treehouse in his younger days. After much engineering effort and countless hours of number crunching on his PC, the project's engineer, Charlie Greenwood, produced a thick and exceedingly complex-looking engineering report and presented it to the building department. It turned out that we did not necessarily need a sympathetic lead inspector. Charlie's report did it. Permission was granted (with a twenty-one-person limit).

Island Wood is a pretty remarkable structure from an engineering standpoint. The main platform is seven-sided and asymmetrical. There are three points of connection to the tree: one where the knee braces come to the trunk (5 to 6 feet off the forest floor); one at the floor level (plus sixteen feet); and the other 28 feet above the floor level, just at the point where the 22-foot-long rafters attach to the tree. It is no wonder that Charlie's calculations got rather intense, as one can imagine how a tree might bend in heavy winds. Not only that, but the connections that Charlie engineered had a double redundancy in that any two points of connection could fail and the remaining single point would be able to support the entire structure. Now that's a piece of engineering! It sure didn't make the building of it any easier, though. Luckily, we had the remarkable skills of Dale West, a carpenter-genius from Port Townsend, Washington, and his trusty assistant, Les Laforge, to wrestle it all together. They did a remarkably fine job, and now Island Wood is a well-used and functional classroom.

ABOVE: *While it was part of the treehouse's program to exclude standard windows, we did manage to incorporate into the design a pair of reclaimed porthole windows from a ship, which were positioned at either side of the view doors.*
OPPOSITE: *The wildly exaggerated roof pitch makes for an interesting look up from inside the treehouse.*

Chapter 4 *Arboriculture: Stuff You Will Want to Know*

For obvious reasons it is extremely important to look into tree care and maintenance before planning a tree-house. After all, the trees are our hosts, and the last thing anyone wants to do is damage or kill them. Each year at the Treehouse Conference in Oregon we have at least two arborists discuss how to go about choosing a healthy tree for treehouse construction and how to keep the tree healthy once the treehouse is attached to it.

Here are some important guidelines to follow:

ROOTS

~ Inspect your tree's roots thoroughly for any sign of possible trouble. A healthy root crown should look like a trumpet set upright on a table resting on its flared bell.

~ Regrading the soil surrounding the tree could actually suffocate its primary buttress roots and compromise the integrity of the tree.

~ Shallow-rooted trees such as beech, oak, or spruce are susceptible to trouble from root compaction resulting from vehicle traffic or heavy foot traffic. Try to avoid compaction by creating an elevated pathway, or spread four-to-six inches of wood chips in the traffic areas.

~ If you suspect trouble with a tree's roots, dig down a few inches to a foot to expose the root flair. Scuff the roots lightly with a chisel to see beneath the bark. A healthy root will be bright pink to red, or green. If disease or decay is found in more than half of the root's circumference, the tree is probably in bad shape and shouldn't even be climbed, much less used to support a treehouse.

~ Many large shade trees can have a healthy-looking canopy as new auxiliary roots compensate for damaged anchoring roots. However, these roots many not be strong enough to keep the tree upright very long in a windstorm, for instance. It is best to avoid these.

TRUNK AND CANOPY

~ Many large mature trees have rotted cores. This does not necessarily rule out the suitability of the tree. If the tree is clearly in the last stages of its life, of course it would be a good idea to avoid it. But in the case of many maples, for instance, even with a partially rotted core, often there is plenty of good wood remaining in the trunk to enable a safe construction. In general, anything less than 8 inches of strong wood "rind" remaining would cause me to want to move on to another tree.

~ Standing water in the "crotch" of a multiple-trunk tree should be left alone, not drained.

~ Exercise caution when building near a section of a tree where two trunks join together at a sharp angle. Check the bark below the connection area to be sure that it is not coming apart. Often this is a good place to install a reinforcing cable at the floor level of the treehouse, or even higher. Having an arborist help with this scenario is a good measure.

~ Inspect the appearance of the canopy. If the leaves or needles are dry and it is not autumn, that could be a sign of trouble.

~ Inspect the base of the trunk for insect infestation. Beetle kill, Dutch elm disease, and gypsy moths periodically ravage trees in the United States, for instance.

PREVENTIVE MEDICINE

~ If the tree passes muster and you intend to build in it, your next challenge is to keep it healthy. Give it a dose of preventive medicine by following these steps:

~ Clear all competing vegetation, especially grass, at the base of the trunk extending out to the circumference of the branches above. Cover the cleared area with 4 to 6 inches of wood chips, and add a bit of tree fertilizer to the mix while you're at it.

- Remove dead wood and snags from among the branches. This will help the tree compensate for the added weight of the treehouse and remove the threat of snags falling onto the treehouse or anyone near it.
- Pruning is strongly encouraged. Do it before you build, and call in an arborist for assistance if you have the least bit of apprehension about it. Pruning, too, will help compensate for the weight of the treehouse and will increase light penetration and air movement while opening up views and reducing wind resistance. If the tree is in a dense forest, don't be afraid to prune neighboring trees for the same purpose. Heck, remove competing trees altogether if it makes sense.
- Trim branches just beyond the collar where it joins the trunk or parent branch. Do not use wound dressing to seal cuts, as this tends to trap moisture against the wound and therefore restrict needed air circulation.

TYPES OF TREES BEST SUITED TO TREEHOUSE CONSTRUCTION
- *Apple:* Classic for kids' treehouses. Easy, low access. Strong. Full of yummy apples for eating and throwing!
- *Ash:* Beautiful when healthy, but watch out for disease when stressed.
- *Banyan:* Grows very fast and will throw your treehouse out of whack quickly, so be prepared. Fun to watch your tree and treehouse intertwine and become one within five years.
- *Fir:* A mature fir is a great treehouse tree. Below a certain level there are not many support branches, so it is often necessary to incorporate more than one tree in the design. Giant firs can even support single-tree designs. Long life span.
- *Hickory:* Extremely hard wood. Tough to bolt onto, but very durable.
- *Madrona:* Very hard wood. Often has multiple trunks enabling interesting designs, but tread lightly: it's sensitive to disease. Use cabling to reinforce trunks. Beautiful, common to U.S. and Canadian west coasts.
- *Mango:* Durable and strong. Has many low branches for easily accessible treehouses. Good for kids' treehouses.
- *Maple:* Durable and fast-growing. Requires careful thinning if mature. Size and softer wood can make it susceptible to storm damage. Sugar maple best of all maples for treehouses because of its plentiful support branches and superior durability.
- *Monkeypod:* Great tree. Perfectly suited for large treehouses. They are strong and durable and consistently form perfect house sites at 25 feet off the ground. Only in your wildest dreams would you be so lucky as to build in one. Native to South America and can be found in Hawaii.
- *Oak:* Very durable, but sensitive to soil compaction and grade changes. The white oak is one of the most beautiful giants in the forest and makes an excellent treehouse host.
- *Palm:* Extremely flexible. Trunk-mount only, and through-bolt all connections. Watch out for falling coconuts!
- *Pine:* Grows fast and straight. Not many support branches. Moderately durable. Caution: Don't pee on it—it's salt intolerant.
- *Spruce:* Medium-density soft wood, but susceptible to insect infestation. Shallow roots. Go with multiple-tree designs for added support.

TYPES OF TREES TO AVOID
- *Alder:* Brittle branches, short life span, prone to infections.
- *Black walnut:* Brittle, branches snap easily.
- *Cottonwood:* Weak-wooded, messy seedpods.
- *Elm:* Prone to many pests and diseases. Often devasted by Dutch elm disease.
- *Sycamore:* Brittle, branches snap easily. Susceptible to insect infestation and disease. Short-lived in urban conditions.

RECOMMENDED JOIST SPANS *Note:* Be sure to check allowable spans between supports and all lumber requirements with your local building department.

Size	Lumber	Spacing	Span
2 x 6	Southern pine or Douglas fir	12" On Center (O.C.)	10'4"
2 x 6	Southern pine or Douglas fir	16" O.C.	9'5"
2 x 6	Southern pine or Douglas fir	24" O.C.	7'10"
2 x 6	Hem-fir	12" O.C.	9'2"
2 x 6	Hem-fir	16" O.C.	8'4"
2 x 6	Hem-fir	24" O.C.	7'3"
2 x 6	Redwood	12" O.C.	8'10"
2 x 6	Redwood	16" O.C.	8'
2 x 6	Redwood	24" O.C.	7'
2 x 8	Southern pine or Douglas fir	12" O.C.	13'8"
2 x 8	Southern pine or Douglas fir	16" O.C.	12'5"
2 x 8	Southern pine or Douglas fir	24" O.C.	10'2"
2 x 8	Hem-fir	12" O.C.	12'1"
2 x 8	Hem-fir	16" O.C.	10'11"
2 x 8	Hem-fir	24" O.C.	8'10"
2 x 8	Redwood	12" O.C.	11'8"
2 x 8	Redwood	16" O.C.	10'7"
2 x 8	Redwood	24" O.C.	8'10"
2 x 10	Southern pine or Douglas fir	12" O.C.	17'5"
2 x 10	Southern pine or Douglas fir	16" O.C.	15'5"
2 x 10	Southern pine or Douglas fir	24" O.C.	12'7"
2 x 10	Hem-fir	12" O.C.	15'4"
2 x 10	Hem-fir	16" O.C.	14'
2 x 10	Hem-fir	24" O.C.	11'7"
2 x 10	Redwood	12" O.C.	14'10"
2 x 10	Redwood	16" O.C.	13'3"
2 x 10	Redwood	24" O.C.	10'10"

MAXIMUM DECKING SPANS *Note:* Be sure to check allowable spans between supports and all lumber requirements with your local building department.

Size	Lumber	Span
5⁄4 x 6	Southern pine or Douglas fir, perpendicular	16"
5⁄4 x 6	Southern pine or Douglas fir, diagonal	12"
5⁄4 x 6	redwood or cedar, perpendicular	16"
5⁄4 x 6	redwood or cedar, diagonal	12"
2 x 4 or 2 x 6	Southern pine or Douglas fir, perpendicular	24"
2 x 4	Southern pine or Douglas fir, diagonal	16"
2 x 6	Southern pine or Douglas fir, diagonal	24"
2 x 4	redwood or cedar, perpendicular	16"
2 x 4 or 2 x 6	redwood or cedar, diagonal	16"
2 x 6	redwood or cedar, perpendicular	24"

GIRDER SPAN OPTIONS *Note:* Be sure to check allowable spans between supports and all lumber requirements with your local building department.

Southern Pine or Douglas Fir

Size of girder	With joists spanning up to	Girder can span up to
4 x 6	6'	6'
4 x 8	6'	8'
4 x 8	8'	7'
4 x 8	10'	6'
4 x 10	6'	10'
4 x 10	8'	8'
4 x 10	10'	7'
4 x 10	12'	7'
4 x 10	14'	6'
4 x 10	16'	6'
4 x 12	6'	11'
4 x 12	8'	10'
4 x 12	10'	9'
4 x 12	12'	8'
4 x 12	14'	7'

Hem-Fir

Size of girder	With joists spanning up to	Girder can span up to
4 x 6	6'	6'
4 x 8	6'	7'
4 x 8	8'	6'
4 x 10	6'	9'
4 x 10	8'	7'
4 x 10	10'	6'
4 x 10	12'	6'
4 x 12	6'	10'
4 x 12	8'	9'
4 x 12	10'	7'
4 x 12	12'	7'
4 x 12	14'	6'

Redwood, Ponderosa Pine, Western Cedar

Size of girder	With joists spanning up to	Girder can span up to
4 x 8	6'	7'
4 x 8	8'	6'
4 x 10	6'	8'
4 x 10	8'	7'
4 x 10	10'	6'
4 x 10	12'	6'
4 x 12	6'	10'
4 x 12	8'	8'
4 x 12	10'	7'
4 x 12	12'	6'
4 x 12	14'	6'

Resources

DESIGN AND CONSTRUCTION

Treehouse Workshop, Inc.
consulting, design, construction,
workshops and GL supplies
2901 W. Commodore Way
Seattle, WA 98199 USA
Phone: (206) 782-0208
Fax: (206) 784-1424
www.treehouseworkshop.com

Barbara Butler, Artist and Builder, Inc.
325 S. Maple Street, #37
San Francisco, CA 94080 USA
Phone: (415) 864-6840
Fax: (650) 877-7223
www.barbarabutler.com

Daniels Wood Land, Inc.
1720 Circle B Road
Paso Robles, CA 93446 USA
Phone: (805) 239-2832
www.danielswoodland.com

Douglas MacGregor, Carver
2536 S. E. Mannthey Rd.
Corbett, OR 97019
(503) 695-5130

Forever Young Treehouses
(Handicap Accessible Treehouses)
178 Main Street, #301
Burlington, VT 05401 USA
Phone: (802) 862-4630
www.treehouses.org

La Cabane Perchée
La Campagne Bertet
84480 Bonnieux, France
www.la-cabane-perchee.com

Living Tree, LLC
Jonathan Fairoaks
Phone: (530) 320-6444
www.livingtreeonline.com

Michael Bock
Hamburg, Germany
michabock@yahoo.com

Michael Garnier
treehouse consulting construction and
GL supplies
www.treehouses.com

Michael Ince
61A Burnett Lane
Brookhaven, NY 11719 USA
(631) 286-5870

Roderick Romero Studios
P.O. Box 737
432 E. Fourteenth Street
New York, NY 10009 USA
www.romerostudios.com

Sahale, LLC
trail & bridge engineering
and construction
Carroll Vogel
P.O. Box 31102
Seattle, WA 98103

T. H. Robandson
Rob van der Wulp
Bussum, Netherlands
www.vanderwulp.net

Treehouse Company
The Stables, Maunsheugh Road
Fenwick, Ayrshire, Scotland KA3 6AN
Phone: +44(0)1560 600111
Fax: +44(0)1560 600110
www.treehouse-company.com

Treehouse Concepts, Kama Lei Cook
Maui, Hawaii
www.treehouseconceptsmaui.com

Treehouse Escapes
Philadelphia, PA USA
www.treehouseescapes.com

Brandon Zebold
metal artist
www.zeboldstudios.com

ENGINEERING

Greenwood Engineering
treehouse engineering and
GL supplies
Charles Greenwood
P.O. Box 1571
Cave Junction. OR 97523 USA
molds@cdsnet.net

LODGING

Cedar Creek Treehouse
P.O. Box 204
Ashford, WA 98304 USA
Phone: (360) 569-2991
www.cedarcreektreehouse.com

Green Magic Treehouse Resort
c/o Palmland Tours
126, Priyadarshini Nagar, Trichur, 5
Kerala, South India
Phone: 0091 487 2420556
www.palmlandtours.net/palmland/tree-house/

Kadir's Yoruk Top Tree House
Olympos, Antalya, Turkey
Phone: +90(0)242 892 12 50
Fax: +90(0)242 892 11 10
www.kadirstreehouses.com

Lothlorien Woods Hide-a-Way
P.O. Box 1697
White Salmon, WA 98672 USA
Phone: (509) 493-TREE
www.lothlorienwoods.com

Out 'n' About Treesort
300 Page Creek Rd.
Cave Junction, OR 97523 USA
Phone: (541) 592-2208
treesort@treehouses.com

Salt Spring Island Hostel
British Columbia, Canada
Phone: (250) 537-4149
www.beacom.com/ssihostel/

Tarzan's House
Ariau Amazon Towers
near Manaus, Brazil
Phone: 877-44ARIAU
www.ariautowers.com

Treehouse Village EcoResort
P.O. Box 506
Kavieng, Papua New Guinea
Phone: (675) 984-2666

Treehouses of Hawaii
P.O. Box 389
Hana, Maui, HI 96713 USA
Phone: (808) 248-7241
www.treehousesofhawaii.com

Waipi'O Treehouse
P.O. Box 5086
Honokaa, HI 96727 USA
Phone: (808) 775-7160

SUPPLIES

American Arborist Supplies Inc
882 South Matlack St.
West Chester, PA 19382
(800) 441-8381
www.arborist.com

Antique and Vintage Woods of America
Pine Planes, NY
www.antiqueandvintagewoods.com
(518) 398-0049

Coldwater Timbers
(seasoned, reclaimed woods)
(206) 799-7678

Fastenal Industrial & Construction
Supplies
www.fastenal.com

New Tribe
(fun tree-climbing supplies)
www.newtribe.com

Pete Nelson's Treehouses,
treehouse books, and supplies.
Send us your best treehouse photos!
PO Box 1136 or
32617 S. E. 44th St.
Fall City, WA 98024
www.petestreehouses.com

Resource Woodworks, Inc.
(salvaged wood)
627 East Sixtieth Street
Tacoma, WA 98404 USA
(206) 474-3757

Used Building Materials Association
www.ubma.org

TREE CARE

Tree Care Industry Association (TCIA)
(formerly the National Association of
Arborists)
www.natlarb.com

OTHER WORTHWHILE ORGANIZATIONS

Circle of Life Foundation
Julia Butterfly Hill
www.circleoflifefoundation.org

Forever Young Treehouses
www.treehouses.org

Hole-in-the-Wall Gang Camp
565 Ashford Center Road
Ashford, CT 06278 USA
Phone: (860) 429-3444
www.holeinthewallgang.org

Make-A-Wish Foundation
www.wish.org

For Further Reading

Alexander, Christopher. *A Pattern Language: Towns, Buildings, Construction.* New York: Oxford University Press, 1977.

Dean, Andrea Oppenheimer and Hursley, Timothy. *Rural Studio: Samuel Mockbee and an Architecture of Decency.* New York: Princeton Architectural Press, 2002.

Nelson, Peter. *Treehouses: The Art and Craft of Living Out on a Limb.* New York: Houghton Mifflin, 1994.

Nelson, Peter. *Home Tree Home: Principles of Treehouse Construction and Other Tall Tales.* New York: Penguin, 1997.

Nelson, Peter and Judy, with David Larkin. *The Treehouse Book.* New York: Universe, 2000.

Stiles, David and Jeanie. *Tree Houses You Can Actually Build.* Boston: Houghton Mifflin, 1998.

Taylor, John. *A Shelter Sketchbook: Timeless Building Solutions.* White River Junction, Vermont: Chelsea Green, 1997.

Index Page numbers in *italics* refer to illustrations.

Index

Acknowledgments

Each of the people listed below has inspired me with his or her integrity and graciousness. I love the idea of emulating the things one admires in others, and in this list the challenge lies before me. Thanks to all of you and especially to Judy, my unwavering and beautiful wife, and Richard Olsen, the man who made this book happen. Richard matched up all the parts and pieces. I am eternally thankful for all his help and encouragement. Thanks also go to graphic designer Bob McKee for creating such an engaging design. A special thank you as well to Jake Jacob, my partner in TreeHouse Workshop. I hope we build together until Olie has to return the two-by-fours.

Anna Daeuble
Tanya and Jeff Jensen
Peter and Lolly Jewett
Julia Butterfly Hill
John Rouches
Ian Jones
Charles Greenwood
Michael Garnier
Marcy Summers
Bubba Smith
Daryl McDonald
Charlie Kellogg
Takashi Kobayashi
Simon Lenton
Paul Rocheleau

Photo Credits

All drawings copyright © 2004 Pete Nelson. All photographs copyright © 2004 Radek Kurzaj, except the following.
Courtesy of Kama Lei Cook/Treehouse Concepts: pp. 202; 203; 204; and 205.
Courtesy of Fur 'n' Feathers Rainforest Treehouses: pp. 170; 171; 172; and 173
Courtesy of David Greenberg/Treehouses of Hawaii: pp. 174; 175; 176; 177; 178; 179; 180; and 181.
Courtesy of John Harris/The Treehouse Company: pp. 126; 127; 128; and 129.
Courtesy of Michael Matisse: pp. 9; 12; 14; 15; 16–17; 18–19; and 20–21.
Courtesy of Pete Nelson: pp. 10–11; 102; 103; 104; 105; 106; 107; 108; 109; 110; 111; 182; 183; 184–185; 186; 187; 188; 189; 190; 191; 192; 193; 194; 195; 196; 197; 198; 199; 200; and 201.
Courtesy of Paul Rocheleau: pp. 74–77.
Courtesy of Manuel Vecchina: pp. 150–153.
Courtesy of Julia Timpanelli O' Dowd: pp. 95–101.
Courtesy of G. Steinmetz: pp. 22; 164; 165; 166; and 167.

Editorial Concept Development,
Project Management, and Editing by Richard Olsen
Designer: Robert McKee
Production Manager: Jane Searle
Copyediting: Richard G. Gallin
Editorial Assistant: Sigi Nacson

Library of Congress Cataloging-in-Publication Data

Nelson, Peter, 1962–
    Treehouses of the world / by Peter Nelson ;
    principal photography by Radek Kurzaj.
                              p. cm.
    Includes bibliographical references and index.
    ISBN 978-0-8109-4952-2 (hardcover)
    1. Tree houses. I. Title.
TH4885.N4723 2004
728'.9—dc22
                              2003027969

Printed and bound in China
10 9 8

HNA
harry n. abrams, inc.
a subsidiary of La Martinière Groupe
115 West 18th Street
New York, NY 10011
www.hnabooks.com